Sikh Cultural Traditions, Customs, Manners and Ceremonies

Sikhism started by Guru Nanak, born in 1469, and the philosophy he propagated has now spread to many parts of the world. The book is one of the first of its kind to highlight the message of the ten Gurus. It also includes the Sikh traditions, culture, customs, manners and ceremonies. Sikhism is one of the natural gifts of India to the world as it is tolerant to other faiths, and believes that everyone is equal and worships the One God (Ik/Ek Omkar), who has been given different names by different religions. Sikhism encourages people to live in peace and also to be tolerant of beliefs and traditions of other faiths. Guru Nanak declared there was only One God (Ik/Ek Omkar), and preached the principal of fatherhood of God and brotherhood of man. Sikhism accepts the doctrine of Karma, transmigration, repetition of the name of God, necessity of the Guru, etc. The book offers everything that its title promises, and also reflects the attitude and beliefs of the Sikhs on matters like the meaning of absolute, Nam Simran etc. It is intended for every one interested in knowing about the traditions, customs, manners and ceremonies of the Sikhs.

Ramesh C. Dogra MBE received his M. Phil. at the University of London and has written twenty books and many articles on many South Asian topics, particularly in the fields of Indology, Sikhism and Bhutan. He retired as Librarian (South Asian Studies), at the School of Oriental and African Studies, University of London in September 2002. In January 2003, New Year's Honour List, in the UK he was awarded MBE (The Most Excellent Order of the British Empire) for his contribution to South Asian Studies.

Mrs. Urmila Dogra, a retired Civil Servant in London, has been associated with the research projects of Mr. Dogra since 1986. She is a co-author of nine books.

The Sikh Cultural Traditions, Customs, Manners and Ceremonies

Ramesh Chander Dogra MBE
Urmila Dogra

DEV PUBLISHERS & DISTRIBUTORS
New Delhi

Published by:
DEV PUBLISHERS & DISTRIBUTORS
2nd Floor, Prakash Deep,
22, Delhi Medical Association Road,
Darya Ganj,
New Delhi-110002
Phone : 011-4357 2647, 98102 36140
e-mail: devbooks@hotmail.com
website: www.devbooks.co.in

ISBN 978–93–81406-24-3
First published 2013

Printed in India

Contents

Introduction

This book is planned to meet a fundamental need to the study of Sikh culture, traditions, customs, manners and ceremonies. Sikhism is one of the natural gifts of India to the world as it is tolerant to other faiths, and believes that everyone is equal and worships the One God (Ik/Ek Omkar), who has been given different names by different religions. India has been a great country of spirituality and mysticism since Vedic times. The Indian people emphasis on spiritual experience in all its forms and has given birth to many religions and also diversity of spiritual teachings, meditation and yogic practices in the world. Sikhism is an integral part of Hindu culture and character. It believes that meditation, remembering the name of God (Nam Simran), and good moral life are the only ways to reach God. Goodness is shown in Sikh actions; Sikhs are expected to help others and always work to support themselves. Sikhism encourages people to live in peace and also to be tolerant of beliefs and traditions of other faiths.

Guru Nanak declared there was only One God (Ik/Ek Omkar), and preached the principal of fatherhood of God and brotherhood of man. Everybody was known as Bhai (brother) or Bebe (sister, mother or elderly woman).

He told people that (a) Vedas, Puran and Quran taught love of humanity; (b) in the eyes of God every person (poor or rich) is equal; (c) taught people to discard rituals and surrender to Lord for peace of mind; (d) and stimulated the people against priesthood, caste system, polytheism and tyranny. He also preached them that their misfortunes were due to their misdeeds in the past life, and assured them that good actions in life would bring them salvation.

Sikhism accepts the doctrine of Karma, transmigration, repetition of the name of God, necessity of the Guru, Bhakti (remembering the Holy Name of God or singing the praises of God with implicit faith and incessant devotion), and rejects Maya (materialism which lures man away from God). The keynote of the Guru's instruction was greater simplicity in belief and worship. Guru Nanak propagated in repetition of God's name, but he gave a new name to God (Ik/Ek Omkar Sat Nam). Guru Nanak wants his follower to repeat the name of such a God who is ever true.

The book offers everything that its title promises, and also reflects the attitude and beliefs of the Sikhs on matters like the meaning of absolute, Nam Simran (remembering the name of God), the function of the Guru Granth Sahib, tradition of Guruship, scriptures, liturgical texts, Rahitnamas, duties of family in performing ceremonies from birth to death. It is intended for general readers, students from School to University level, and also for Sikh/ Hindu people and other readers who are interested in knowing about the traditions, customs, manners and ceremonies of the Sikhs. We hope that this book will be useful to all those interested in the subject.

RAMESH CHANDER DOGRA MBE & URMILA DOGRA

1

The Sikh and Singh, Gurdwara, Gurus, GGS and Dasam Granth

The Sikh

In Panjabi, Sikh/Sikhna means studying, learning, hence a Sikh means a learner or a disciple, or a follower of Guru Nanak and the other nine Gurus. The main distinction between a Sikh and a Singh is that all the Singhs are Sikhs, but all the Sikhs are not Singhs. Only those Sikhs who take the Pahul (baptism) initiated by the tenth Guru, Gobind Singh, are known as Singhs. Guru Nanak, a religious preacher of saintly disposition, who preached harmony with secular life, founded the Sikh religion. The Guru's mission in life was to reconcile the Hindus and Muslims and to enable them to live together in peace. It was this ideal which he followed throughout his life. It represented his vision of harmony, tolerance and co-operation for mankind and its ultimate union with the Divine. He died in 1539 after nominating his devoted disciple Guru Angad (1539-1552), as his successor excluding his two sons. Guru Angad and the next Guru, Amar Das (1552-1574), were men of great ability and saintly disposition. Guru Amar Das was succeeded in the Guru's office by his son-in-law Ram Das (1574-1881). Under the fifth Guru Arjan Dev (1581-1606) the Sikh community grew in numbers and spread far and wide over the Panjab.

He compiled the Adi Granth (the first sacred book of the Sikhs). He tried to organise the finances of Gurdwaras by introducing the system of spiritual tribute to be collected by his agents called Masands. The next guru, Guru Hargobind (1606-1644), son of Guru Arjan Dev, was a man of warlike and adventurous spirits. He maintained an army, carried two swords, and taught Sikhs to defend their faith. He died in 1645 after nominating his younger grandson, Har Rai (1644-1661), as his successor. The eighth Guru Har Krishan (1661-1664) was the second son of the seventh guru, and at the age of five he became the child guru.

After the death of Guru Har Krishan in 1664, there were quarrels about succession to the Guruship, but Guru Tegh Bahadur (1665-1675) the second son of Guru Hargobind (the sixth Guru) was nominated as the Guru. He protested against certain measures of the Emperor and encouraged Kashmiri Hindus to resist these. He was beheaded, for upholding the principle of freedom of conscience, on order of Emperor Aurangzeb. Thus he gave his head but not his faith as he was offered the choice between death and conversion.

Guru Gobind Singh (1675-1708), the tenth and last guru, was the son and successor of Guru Tegh Bahadur. He was one of the most remarkable personalities in Indian history. He knew many languages and was scholar of Sanskrit and Persian and a military genius. He created the Khalsa order. Those who accepted his new form of baptism were known as Khalsa (pure) and were given the appellation of Singh (lion). An Afghan fanatic stabbed him to death, towards the end of 1708, at Nader, on the banks of river Godavari. The cruelty of Muslim rulers towards Sikhs and Hindus turned them, under tenth guru, Guru Gobind Singh, from a band of religious devotees into a chosen religious and military commonwealth of Khalsa.

After the death of Guru Gobind Singh, Banda Bahadur, a devotee of Guru Gobind Singh, became the leader of the Guru's army (Khalsa). Banda Bahadur returned to the

Panjab, bearing all the essential tokens of Sikh leadership, including five arrows from the Guru's own quiver, a flag (nishan), a drum (nagara), five duly appointed aides (Piyaras—who constituted a Panchayat) and a guard of twenty other Singhs. He had also a Hukamanama (warrant) from the Guru Gobind Singh, bidding all the Sikhs to support him. He offered the Sikhs a new battle cry, "Fatah Darshan" (victory to the revelation). Banda proclaimed himself to be the protector of the poor against all tyrants and robbers, and promised all who co-operated in the Khalsa cause, a share in fruits of conquest. Banda proceeded to wage an open and relentless war on the Mughals. He punished the Mughals for the execution of Guru Tegh Bahadur and bricking alive the two young sons of Guru Gobind Singh.

The Mughals were frightened of Banda Bahadur and he won one city after the other, and became the ruler of Panjab from Delhi to Lahore. This was the first in the history of Gurus that the Sikhs became the rulers of Panjab.

This victory was not long to live, as the Mughals were successful in dividing the Sikhs, because Guru Gobind Singh's widow ex-communicated Banda Bahadur. The Sikh army was divided into two armies, his followers being called Bandai Sikhs and other were called Tat Khalsa. This led to the weakening of the army and Banda was captured at the siege of Gurdaspur and was killed mercilessly.

Towards the end of the eighteenth century, the Sikhs became dominant again and their influence extended from Kara-Kuram Mountains to the plains of Sind, and from Peshawar to Delhi.

Singh, distinctive features

Unshorn hairs and a blue dress, as the characteristics of a believer, do not appear as direct injunctions in any extant writing attributed to Guru Gobind Singh, and they seem chiefly to have derived their distinction as marks from custom or usage, while propriety of wearing a blue dress is now regarded as less obligatory than formerly. Both usages have originated in a spirit of opposition to Islam, for many Muslims keep their heads shorn, and many Hindu saints keep their unshorn hairs including all the Hindu deities. It is also curious, with regard to colour, Nihangs and many Hindus think that God likes the blue colour and that is why the sky, the purified flames of a fire and the water— all are blue. Lord Shiva is also blue-necked and he is auspicious and also the first divine physician. Rudra is another name of Shiva. In Rig-Vedas word Rudra is used for Agni (fire), which produces blue flames. Lord Krishna and his brother Balram is also described as wearing blue clothes.

The Singh or a Sikh should refrain from tobacco and drugs, although tobacco itself seems to have been originally included as snuff only among proscribed things. Tobacco was first introduced into India about 1617.

Another difference, which may be noticed, is that a Singh of Guru Gobind Singh would also wear Kanga (comb), Kara (steel bangle), Kachch or underpants or drawers and Kirpan (steel sword). Many Hindu also wear Kachha and Kara now a days. A Singh may be distinguished from Hindus chiefly by a higher topknot of hair and usually turban on top of that.

Guru Granth Sahib/Adi Granth as Supreme authority in Sikhism

Sikhism is one of the natural gifts of India to the mankind as it is tolerant to other faiths, and believes that everyone is equal and worships the One God, who has been given different names by different religions. It is an integral part of Indian character. It believes that meditation, remembering the name of God, and good moral life are the only ways to reach God. It is apparent that the Guru Granth Sahib is the supreme authority in Sikhism and one should be able to find all the answers concerning the Sikh religion in it. The Granth comprises writings of Guru Nanak and the succeeding teachers of the Sikh faith up to the ninth Guru, omitting, the sixth, seventh and eighth. Secondly, the composition of certain Bhagats or saints, mostly sectarian

Hindus, sixteen in number, Thirdly, the verses of certain 'Bhagats' followers of Nanak and his successors.

It is believed that the text of the Granth by different people may be subject to different interpretations by different people. Secondly the Granth says nothing about Rahit Namas (code of conduct) except the Five Ks and the initiation ceremony by the last Guru Gobind Singh. There are many Sikhs who do not observe all the Five Ks. It is only during the latter half of the nineteenth century that the Singh Sabha reformist movement emerged and it began to compile a manual of Rahit Nama, which was finally issued in 1915 as a Sikh code of conduct.

In 1873 Singh Sabha was established in Amritsar to reform and secure absolute control and declare itself as the supreme authority in Sikhism. The more distinguished members broke away and established another Singh Sabha at Lahore. The objects of Lahore Singh Sabha were to interpret more truly the teachings of the Granth. Due to internal quarrels the Khalsa Diwan was set up in 1883 as the supreme authority. Discussion between different parties continued and as a result of that Chief Khalsa Diwan was founded in 1902. The objects of the Diwan were to issue religious and secular instructions for the reformation and improvement of the Sikh community. For various reasons the Diwan could not continue as it was not acceptable to the orthodox Sikh community and to the religious authorities of the Amritsar Golden temple.

The Shiromani Gurdwara Prabandhak Committee (SGPC) was formed due to the Gurdwaras Act of 1925. The Act allowed the SGPC to be the supreme authority for the interpretation of the Granth within the supremacy of the Adi Granth/Guru Granth Sahib. Many Sikhs did not question the supremacy of the Granth, but did not accept the supreme authority of the SGPC due to the manner in which it elects its members and Jathedar (commander). Many Sikhs believe that the structure of the SGPC and its election is unsatisfactory. Some believe that the ordinary people in every assembly should elect its Panj Payaras (five representatives) and they should be the supreme or final authority in the interpretation of the Granth.

The Sikhs believe that the Guru Granth Sahib is the final and the only authority, and the SGPC and other institutions should keep on changing their rules and regulations with the time according to the instructions of the holy scriptures.

God (Parbrahm)—definition according to Sikhism

Sikhism is a theistic faith and firmly asserts that God is the one and sole Supreme Reality. God as described by Guru Nanak in the Mul-mantra (Japji):

God is One, His name is True. He is ever existing, Fearless, Inimical to none, Unborn, Deathless, Self-existent, Self-illuminated and Ever True. He is the creator of all that is seen or unseen. He will live forever. God is the only giver whatever one possesses and enjoys. Other definition of God in the Guru Granth Sahib and Dasam Granth are as follows:

God has no worries, no parents, and His creations are limitless. God manifests himself in everything, including, beggar, donor, master, servant etc. God is the cause of all joy and, and the cause of everything that controls us all in this universe. God is the only true giver of everything. He nourishes us All, resides in us and protects all of us. God is the Supreme Lord of all and He speaks in all the living beings. World exists at God's command. One gets rewards and punishments according to one's deeds (Karma). God created the universe, the planets, the Sun and the Stars, and millions of creatures. He bestowed special favours on man, granting the faculty to reason about the purpose of life, and the freedom of action to seek self-realisation. The goal of man is to escape from the cycle of births and deaths and for the soul to mingle with the Creator. God's realisation is possible through Sahaj Marg/Bhakti emphasising prayers, meditation and good deeds.

Guru in Sikhism

Literally, the word Guru means an enlightener: (Gu means darkness, Ru means light), one who provides light in darkness. The Guru tradition had been quite strong in India. The Guru means a religious teacher and a guide throughout his/her disciple's life. During the Bhakti movement, Guru Nanak used the word 'Satguru' (Primal Guru) for God, his own Guru, The Guru may serve two purposes: he may provide religious and moral teachings, and also supervise his progress throughout his life. The Guru shows the righteous way to every one. Without carrying out the instructions of the Guru, no one can obtain salvation. The Guru is like a fountain of nectar to satisfy the thirst of the seeker of Truth with the Lord's Holy Name.

The words and teachings of the Guru are called Gurmat. The hymns of the Guru provide guidance and inspiration to the seeker of Truth. The Guru takes the disciple through the pace of sunan (hearing the holy word), manna (acceptance of the faith of the holy word), and nidhasan (meditation). He proceeds from the plane of piety to the planes of true knowledge, spiritual effort, divine grace, till he enters the Realm of Truth, where he establishes a permanent link with God.

In Sikh religion, the Guru stands for God as, for example, God was the Guru Nanak. Secondly, Guru stands for the Ten Gurus who, as messengers of God, imparted spiritual knowledge to their followers. Thirdly, Guru means the teachings of the Guru or his hymns—Bani (the revelation of the holy spirit). Fourthly, Guru stands for the congregation or the body of Sikhs in prayer (Guru sangat) or in the baptised fraternity of the Khalsa.

The qualities of the true Guru are mentioned in the Sikh scriptures. He is selfless, virtuous and humble. He is free from vice; his company is inspiring and spiritually uplifting; he is source of joy and bliss to his disciples.

Gurus—treated as one Nanak

Guru Nanak is generally said to have been born in Talwandi, a village on river Ravi near Lahore. But one manuscript account states that, although the father of the Guru was of Talwandi, the teacher himself was born in Kanakatch, about fifteen miles southerly from Lahore, in the house of his mother's parents. It is indeed not uncommon in the Panjab and many other parts of India for women to choose their own parents' home as the place of their confinement, especially of their first child, and the children thus born are frequently called Nanak (or Nanaki, in the feminine), from Nanke, from one's mother's parents. Nanak is thus a name of usual occurrence, both among Hindus and Muslims.

Guru Nanak's meeting and dialogues with the Yogis or Kanphatas are mentioned in the Granth and the Janam Sakhis. The idea of Guru and the spiritual succession was also very common among these Yogis or the Siddas and among all the Hindu sects. It is believed that without the Guru one is not destined to achieve enlightenment. Guru is not only a religious teacher, but also a guide to his disciple throughout his life.

The idea of spiritual succession was quite common among Hindus and it also came into Buddhism and Sufi Muhammadans from the Hindus.The idea has developed from the theory of incarnation among the Hindus. The important element of the concept is not the spiritual succession but spiritual transmission. The belief of unity in the plurality of the Gurus served a useful purpose in the development of Sikhism. Therefore all the Sikhs Gurus were known as the Nanak the First, Nanak the Second, Nanak the Third etc.

Gurdwara

A Sikh temple or shrine is called a Gurdwara, that is, the House of God, the House of Guru. Its most essential element is the presence of the Guru Granth Sahib. According to Sikhism, prayers to God can be offered at any time and anywhere; a Gurdwara is built particularly for congregational worship. Most of their important shrines are connected with the ten Gurus and are great centres of pilgrimage.

The Gurdwara is open to all castes and no purdah is observed. In the house of the Lord, all are equal, irrespective of their status in the world outside. On a visit to the Gurdwara, the head is kept covered as a mark of respect to the Guru Granth Sahib, and shoes are not allowed inside the temple. Liquor, other intoxicants and smoking are not allowed. All Gurdwaras employ priests (Granthis), so that someone can devote all his time to the upkeep of the temple. In the earlier days many decisions affecting the social and political life of the community used to be taken in the Gurdwara through a consensus of the sangat (congregation). These decisions, called Gurmattas, were of a binding character, and an ember of the community would think twice before violating them. Many important decisions were taken at Akal Takht, Amritsar. There are four other historical shrines given the status of Takhts (thrones) where the decisions taken by the Sangat (congregation) had great importance. These are Harmandar Sahib (Patna), Keshgarh Sahib (Anandpur), Damdama Sahib (Talwandi Sabo), and Hazur Sahib (Nander, Maharashtra).

The first Gurdwara was set up by Guru Nanak at Kartarpur in 1521. It serves as a centre for training in spiritual knowledge and wisdom. It offers food and shelter to any one who needs it. It provides care for the poor, the sick and the aged. Besides prayer, hymn singing and sharing food, it promoted literacy and training in martial arts for the defence of those who need it. There is no particular design in building Gurdwara. It may be any style of architecture. However, some Gurdwaras in the Panjab have been built on a common plan of a doomed structure with a main hall for the congregation, rooms for the caretakers and the visitors, and adequate place for a kitchen, toilet and dining hall.

The Gurdwara serves as a community centre, and apart from weekly congregation on Saturday and Sunday, it may provide some of the following services:

(1) Teaching of the Panjab language. (2) Kirtan classes. (3) Discussion groups on Sikhism. (4) Publication and distribution of books on Sikhism. (5) Library service, and aid to the needy people. (6) Congregation for ladies and employment for needy women. (7). About immigration, maintaining contacts with local police and prison services. (8). Youth activities and indoor games, hobbies and sports. (9) Day centre for old people and dispensary or clinic for the sick.

Gurdwara Income—from offerings or Daswand (one-tenth of income)

Some of the Gurus made it compulsory for every devotee to pay a part of their earnings to the Guru for construction and welfare projects. One of the greatest factors in an established Gurdwara is the priestly class, which works either for the superstructure or its downfall and, as history tells us, generally for the latter. Sikh Gurus adopted precautionary measures against any such collapse. Guru Nanak said that the income from offerings was like poison and incapable of being digested except through constant prayers and devotion. A priest should take only so much, as is barely sufficient for his maintenance. And those who live on it would be subjected to many hardships here in this world and will be sent to the hell in the next.

In Nanak Prakash of Bhai Santokh Singh it is mentioned. Part 9, Ras 9:

Everyone should hear that income from offerings should never be used for personal benefits. Anyone, who uses the income for personal gain, shall become a dog in their next life.

Bhai Desa Singh in his Rahatnama says:

A good Sikh should always earn money by doing some work. He should never accept offerings. A Sikh who is acting as a priest, should not accept more than what is barely sufficient for his maintenance. If more were offered it should be given away in charity.

The Sikhs Gurus accepted the offerings in kind and cash for running the Langar (free kitchen) and for the construction of Gurdwaras.

Guru Arjan (1581-1606) after becoming the Guru needed money to complete the construction of both the tanks and temples left unfinished by his father. The Guru made it compulsory for every devotee to pay one-tenth of their earnings to the Guru for religious purposes, construction and welfare projects. According to Rahat-nama, it is compulsory for the Sikh to donate Daswand (one-tenth of income) for charitable and religious purposes. For collecting money he nominated some Jat Sikhs as Masands. The Masands were not paid a salary, but they retained one-third of the money and other offerings received from the Sikhs. The Masands collected offerings regularly and paid them to the Guru on Diwali and Baisakhi days. This was a great source of income for the construction of the buildings and welfare programmes. The tank Amrit Sarovar (The Pool of Nectar) was finished in 1588, and Raja of Mandi (Himachal Pradesh) paid Rs. 4,000 for its construction. The Guru encouraged his devotees to engage in trade and commerce in addition to agriculture. Many of his devotees started trading in horses, which were bought from Central, and West Asia and sold in India. He also organised some trade in horses for himself to meet his personal expenses. He did not live on the offerings of his devotees.

The offerings became compulsory from the time of Guru Arjan. During the time of Guru Gobind Singh the money was needed to buy arms and horses and to maintain some army to fight the Mughals. The Guru told his followers to keep a pot at home to keep money for charity. He instructed his followers to empty the pot on Diwali, Baisakhi and Holi days and give the money personally to the Guru. The Guru did not trust Masands who were appointed by Guru Arjan for collecting the money. During the time of Guru Gobind (10th Guru) the Masands became dishonest and therefore he abolished the system of collecting money by the Masands.

In order to celebrate the festivals (Diwali, Lohri, and Baisakhi) the Guru issued orders to his devotees and asked them to meet him on the auspicious days of the festivals. It served a dual purpose of receiving offerings personally and celebrating the festivals with his devotees.

It is believed in Hinduism and Sikhism that a man who gains wealth without work is a spoilt man. He becomes indolent and sluggish both in physical and intellectual work. The priest should not form a separate class, and their descendants should not live on offerings alone. They should acquire income from other means, as was the case during the Vedic period.

Langar (Free kitchen)

Langar or free kitchen is the Guru's way of combining worship with food. The Gurdwara is both the temple of prayer and the temple of bread. The community mess (refractory) is a practical institution to demonstrate the principle of sharing our earnings with others. Guru Amar Das made the Langar an integral part of the Sikh temple by providing accommodation for the kitchen, dining hall and a pantry (for stocking food stuffs). The Langar is the joint responsibility of the Sikh community and does not depend on the charity of outsiders. Guru Gobind Singh directed his followers to maintain Linger in their own homes, for he declared: "May the kitchen and sword prevail in the world".

Langar is a place of training in voluntary service and the practice of philanthropy and equality. Service is involved in the collection of fuel and rations, cutting of vegetables, cooking of food, distribution of meals, serving of drinking water, washing of utensils and dishes, and the cleaning of dining halls. It is a practical demonstration of hospitality and love of human beings. Secondly, the Langar ensures social equality and integration. It is the most effective step of removing caste prejudice and exclusiveness. It is a means of improving the lot of the untouchables, and for treatment of the poor and the underprivileged. It proclaims the dignity of an ordinary human being, based on the equality of men and women without any prejudice to caste or creed.

The Sikh community is under an obligation to maintain a Langar in the Gurdwara. Voluntary donations or Daswand (one-tenth of income) support the Langar. In the case of historical Gurdwaras, the land allotted to them yields enough grains and vegetables on its own, or if the land is given on lease, it can yield income sufficient to meet the requirements of the food purchased from the market. Maharaja Ranjit Singh made endowments of land and properties to many Gurdwaras to enable them to discharge their services to the community. Only vegetarian food is provided in the Langar. Many people who arrange Kirtan programmes or Akhand Paths in their homes serve vegetarian food (Langar) at the end of the function. It is mentioned in the Sikh prayer that food and water belong to God and the desire to serve the people gives pleasure to the Sikhs.

Food

The ordinary food of the Sikh peasants consists of Chapatis (made from wheat flour, or barley, or jowar i.e. millet) and they are eaten with Daal (made from split pea of gram, or mungi, masur, motth, harhar etc) and any vegetable available during the season. Salt is always used and red pepper and spices are generally added for seasoning. The whole is washed down with lassi (buttermilk). Carrots, turnips, onions and pumpkins may be eaten, but the favourite substitute for vegetable is Sarson-ka-saag. Sarson-ka-sag and Makki ki roti

(Indian corn—bread) are the most favourite meal of the Sikhs and Panjabis. Sugar and gur (raw sugar) appears in various forms at marriages and other festive occasions, but foods like ghi (clarified butter) are used as much as one can afford. The heaviest meal is taken in the house at sundown, when the work of the day is over. The cooking is mostly done by women.

Eating of flesh was not allowed by any Guru except Guru Gobind Singh who allowed them during the wartime when vegetarian food was not available, and they were allowed to kill a wild animal and eat. Meat is eaten by people who can afford it. They eat Jhatka meat (decapitation by a blow at the back of the head). They do not eat Halal meat of Muslims. Beef is unholy to the Sikhs, but there is no objection to sheep, goat and pig. The Kara Parshad (sacramental food) is a standing dish at all religious ceremonies, at festive occasions and happy times.

Wine/Liquor and Tobacco

Sikhism rejects the use of intoxicants and drugs. Their use is physically harmful and mentally injurious. Alcohol and drugs are prohibited to Sikhs in their Holy Books. In the Adi Granth (Bihagre Ki Var) there are three Salokas (couplets) of Guru Nanak dedicated to Mardana, against the use of wine. Guru Amar Das says (Adi Granth p. 553) that by drinking wine/liquor one earns the wages of vice and sin. Guru Har Gobind said that wine is evil and one who drinks it loses his senses. Guru Tegh Bahadur instructed his devotees not to use wine and tobacco. Guru Gobind Singh told his followers that if any one cuts his hair, use tobacco and wine, associate with a woman other than his own wife, or ate the Halal meat of Muslims, will be excommunicated from the Khalsa. He must be re-baptised to enter into the Khalsa community, after repenting about his sins.

Sikh Gurus

Guru's name	Birth	Installation as Guru	Death
1. Guru Nanak	15.4.1469		22.9.1539
2. Guru Angad	31.3.1504	14.6.1539	29.3.1552
3. Guru Amar Das	5.5.1479	29.3.1552	1.9.1574
4. Guru Ram Das	24.9.1534	1.9.1574	1.9.1581
5. Guru Arjan	15.4.1563	1.9.1581	30.5.1606
6. Guru Hatgobind	14.6.1595	25.5.1606	3.3.1644
7. Guru Har Rai	26.2.1630	8.3.1644	6.10.1661
8. Guru Har Krishan	7.7.1656	7.10.1661	30.3.1664
9. Guru Tegh Bahaduer	1.4.1621	20.3.1665	11.11.1675
10.Guru Gobind Singh	22.12.1666	11.11.1675	7.10.1708

Nanak, Guru (15.4.1469—22.9.1539)

Nanak was born at Rae Bhoi Ki Talwandi known as Nankana Sahib in Sheikhupura district (now Pakistan). His father's name was Kalu Ram and his mother's name was Tripta. He belonged to the Bedi Gotra (lineage) of Kshatriyas. The word Bedi or Vedi originally meant, those who had studied only one Veda as compared with Dwivedi, Trivedi and Chaturvedi. Kalu Ram was a shopkeeper as well as the village Patwari or record keeper for the local landlord, Rae Bular Bhatti, a recent convert to Islam. Nanak learnt arithmetic and accountancy in Lande Mahajani from his father, reading and writing in Devnagari from a Pandit, and Persian and Arabic from a Muslim teacher.

When Nanak was only five years old the sister of Nanak's mother, Bibi Lakho, came to see her sister Nanki and observed Nanak's indifference to worldly affairs. She remarked that Nanak would become a saint. Nanak replied that she would also have a saint. Thus Nanak predicted the birth of the famous saint Baba Ram Thamman whose shrine is at the place of that name near Kasur.

As a child Nanak was devoted to the meditation of God, and at the age of seven he was sent to the Hindu village school, where he composed 35 verses, which were later included in the Rag Asa of the Guru Granth Sahib. He was a gifted child who learnt everything thoroughly and quickly.

His understanding of spiritual things amazed his teachers. At the age of nine, Nanak was invested with the sacred thread of the twice born Hindu. Nanak spent much of time in solitude and meditation.

Nanak always felt happier in the company of Hindu and Muslim saints. He did not want to become like his father and devoted all his time in uttering God's name. Nanaki, elder sister of Nanak, took Nanak to Sultanpur Lodi in Jalandhar. Jai Ram Uppal, husband of Nanki, got Nanak the post of a storekeeper. Nanak worked honestly, but his mind was always singing the praises of God. Out of jealousy, his colleagues made a complaint, that Nanak was squandering the stores by giving free rations to poor people and holy men. An enquiry cleared him of any malpractice. He resigned and devoted himself to spiritual pursuits.

At the age of eighteen Nanak was married to Sulakhani, daughter of Mulchand Chona Khatri of Pakhoke. Married life had no attraction to Nanak though he had two sons, Sri Chand born in 1494 and Lakhmi Das born in 1496. When he left home to spread his message, the duty of looking after Nanak's wife and children fell on his sister and brother-in-law. His wife however rejoined him after his travels and lived with him till his death.

Nanak visited daily Kali Bein, a river flowing nearby. He found that men and women of the town bathed in that river daily in the month of Kartik. He also went to the river daily to have a bath and to recite hymns to some people. One day he took shelter in a cave in the bank of the river and fell into a trance. He remained there for three days and had a Revelation, a mystic vision of God's court where he was commanded to propagate the Holy Name. He proclaimed his mission: the Fatherhood of God, the Brotherhood of Man, and the Motherhood of Nature. After this event Guru Nanak took the decisive step of distributing all that he had among the poor and left his house and began to preach.

Nanak's message was "Na koi Hindu na koi Musalman". He said that there were no Hindus or Muslims and we were all human beings, sons and daughters of the same Supreme Being. He said that people could not be divided on the basis of religion. He wanted Hindus and Muslims to live together in peace and tranquillity. His first pronouncement "There is no Hindu and No Musalman" led to his being cited, at the Qazi's instance, to appear before the Nawab, who invited him to accompany him to the mosque. Nanak did so—and while the Qazi led the prayers, he laughed. To the Qazi's remonstration he replied that the latter had left a foal in his own courtyard and throughout the prayers had been anxious lest it should fall into the well. Amazed at the Nanak's power of reading his thoughts the Qazi fell at his feet and acknowledged his power.

In 1499 Nanak started his missionary work and Mardana, the village minstrel joined him. It became usual for both of them to sing songs in the praise of God in the morning and evening, before and after office hours, in a public place. Mardana lived with Nanak all his life and played sweet music on his rebeck when Nanak sang hymns in the praise of God.

Of Nanak's life, few authentic details are available in a Janamsakhi (biography), assigned by E. Trumpp, called Walayat Wali Janamsakhi. This biography (Janamsakhi) contains few of the miracles and other incidents found in the later Janamsaskhis, and may be regarded as an authentic biography.

Nanak undertook four missionary tours and covered more than 20,000 miles in 14 years. The first tour was in Eastern India and preached people three rules of life:

i. One should earn one's livelihood and maintain one's family.
ii. One should share their food and give money in charity to the poor.
iii. One should remember God while leading an honest life.

During his second tour the Guru went to the South of India and visited Ceylon (Sri Lanka) and its ruler became his great admirer. The third tour took him to the Himalayas, where he held discussions with the Yogis. These are recorded in one of his compositions called Sidh Gosht. During his fourth tour, the Guru visited western India, Mecca, and Baghdad.

Nanak went on pilgrimage to Mecca, where by chance he lay down and turned his feet towards the Kaba. When reproached for by the Qazi, Rukn-ud-Din, he challenged him to lay his feet in any direction where God's house did not lie, and wherever the Qazi turned Nanak's feet, the Kaba appeared. He fell at his feet and asked forgiveness.

He went to Gorakh-hatri where he discoursed with the 84 Sidhs (disciples of Gorakh Nath). A temple exists at Nanakmata in the Kuamon. Not far from this place there still can be found several maths of Yogis. When the Guru visited Eminabad he meditated on a bed of pebbles where the Rori Sahib now stands. Here he composed a hymn in which he reproached the disciples of Gorakh Nath for subsisting on alms wrung from the people and expounded the merits of earning a livelihood by honest labour.

Nanak, Guru —and Babar's invasion 1520-1524.

In the winter of 1520-21, after a visit to Mecca, Guru Nanak was returning home from Baghdad through Khurasan and Afghanistan. He noticed that many young men, in these places, with horses and arms were joining Babar to invade India. The Guru followed the traditional route via Heart, Kandhar, Ghazni, Kabul, Jalalabad, Khaibar Pass, Peshawar and Attock. The Guru was also known as Haji as he had made a pilgrimage to Mecca. At Hasan Abdal he was greatly honoured by the people as Haji. At the request of the people he left a print of his palm near a spring. A Gurdwara was later built in the Guru's memory at that spot, and it was known as Panja Sahib. On the way he spent some time with his old disciple, Bhai Lalo, who complained to the Guru about the oppression of Lodi kings, their officials and Pathans in general. The Guru replied that their rule would end soon as Babar was going to invade India. The Guru was still at Sayyidpur when Babar entered the Panjab. At that time Hindu traders and landlords inhabited most of the towns in Panjab. They offered considerable resistance to Babar to save their lives, honour and property. Babar did not like their resistance and ordered a general massacre of the people. The Guru says that all the young women were made slaves, and the older ones were forced to grind corn and cook food for the troops. People were robbed of their property and then their houses were burnt. Guru Nanak and Lalo were forced to carry heavy loads of looted property on their heads to the army camp and then forced to grind corn. The town Sayyidpur was renamed Eminabad. The horrible treatment of Hindu women disturbed the Guru very much, but he could not do anything to save them from dishonour and slavery. In his four hymns called Babar Vani, the Guru says about Babar's cruelty:

Thou, O Creator of all things,
Thou hast struck terror at the heart of Hindustan through the ruler of Khurasan;
Takest to Thyself no blame;
Thou hath sent Yam (God of death) disguised as the great Moghal Babar.
Terrible was the slaughter,
Loud were the cries of the sufferers,
Did this not awaken pity in Thee, O Lord?
Aiti mar pai kurlane tain ki dard na aiya
Thou art part and parcel of all things equally, O Creator;
Thou must feel for all men and all nations.
If a strong man attacks another who is equally strong;
Where is the grief in this, or whose is the grievance?
But when a fierce tiger preys on the helpless cattle,
The herdsman must answer for it.

Treatment of women by Babar—described by Guru Nanak:
The pitiable condition of captive women
The tresses that adorned these lovely heads,
And were parted with vermilion,
Have been shorn with cruel shears;
Dust has been thrown on their shaven heads.
Hey lived in ease in palaces,
Now they must beg by the roadside,
Having no place for their shelter.

When these whose heads are shorn were married,
Fair indeed seemed their bridegrooms beside them.
They were brought home in palanquins carved with ivory,
Pitchers of water were waved over their heads, in ceremonial welcome.
Ornate fans flittered waving above them.
At the first entry into the new home,
Each bride was offered a gift of a lakh of rupees,
Another lakh when each stood up to take her post in her new home;
Coconut shredding and raisins were among the delicious fruits,
Served to them at their tables.
These beauties lent charm to the couches they reclined on.
Now they are dragged away with ropes round their necks;
Their necklaces are snapped and their pearls scattered.
Their beauty and wealth are their greatest enemies now;
Barbarous soldiers have taken them prisoners and disgraced them.
Few, some very few, from this have return home,
And others enquire of them about their lost dear ones.
Many are lost forever,
And weeping and anguish are the lot of those who survive.

Guru Nanak says that rape was committed indiscriminately. The women who suffered were Hindustani, Turkani, Bhatiani and Thakaurani. (Rag Asa. p.417.)

Guru Nanak says that in the winter of 1524 Babar attacked Lahore and captured the city and thoroughly sacked it. Nanak observed:

Lahore shahar, zaihar, qaihar, sawa paihar
(Lahore city was given over to death and violence for four hours)
In Var Malhar (Adi Granth p.1288) Guru Nanak says:
Raje sinh, muqaddam kutte (kings are tigers and officials are dogs)

In Sarang the Guru says:
Kali hoi kutte muhi khaju hoya murdar
(In this Kali age men are behaving like dogs that eat carrion.)
Nanak further says: sin is the king, greed the minister, falsehood the mint master, and lust the deputy to take counsel with. The blind subjects, out of ignorance, pay homage like dead men.

Successors of Guru Nanak

Angad, Guru, (1539-1552), Second Guru, Guru Angad who was earlier called Lahna, born at Matte di Sarai in Ferozpur District on 31 March 1504 in a shopkeeper's family. He was a man of simple beliefs and devoted to Goddess Durga. From his village Khadur he used to visit the Durga temple at Jawalamukhi regularly. Once on his way to the Durga temple, Lahna heard about a saint called Guru Nanak. He heard a hymn of the Guru being sung by some people. He was charmed by the melody and significance of the hymns. On enquiry, he learnt that the saint Nanak was living in Kartarpur. He went to Kartarpur to pay his regards to the saint and became his disciple for good. The Sikh tradition states, that Nanak changed the name Lahna into that of Angad (one's own limb or part of body) when conferring on him the Guruship, as being a part of himself. He served the Guru from 1539 to 1552 and was nominated by the Guru as his successor.

All the Sikh Gurus call themselves "Nanak" in order to designate themselves as the successors or part of Guru Nanak. For the sake of distinction between them in the Adi Granth (Mahalla pahila, first chapter or Pahili Patshahi, first reign etc) is mentioned. The Sikhs looked on their Gurus as sovereigns. In later times, when Guru Nanak was gradually looked upon as an Avtar (incarnation), every succeeding Guru was considered as an incarnation of Baba Nanak

He shifted from Kartarpur to Khadur in Amritsar in order to avoid the conflict with the Guru's sons. During the first six months he remained hidden in the house of a devotee. At the request of Bhai Buddha he resumed the responsibilities of the office of the Guru. He learnt the Adi Granth and worked in the langar (free kitchen). He was totally obedient to his Guru and such won his confidence.

The Guru's selection might be due to the fact that he was more intelligent than others and faithful to Guru. Nanak. Guru Nanak had rejected the claims of his eldest son Sri Chand because he came out inferior to Lahna in his devotion to the Guru and also he had ascetic tendency. The younger son Lakshmi Das was not interested in becoming Guru. Many Sikhs became the followers of Sri Chand and were called Udasis.

He decided to collect the hymns of Guru Nanak, which were written in the local language (Lande Mahajani) or committed to memory by some of Nanak's disciples, especially Bhai Bala. Guru Angad being the son of a village shopkeeper knew Lande Mahajani script. In writing its vowel sounds are omitted and can be misread e.g., (Guru ji Ajmer gai han (Guru Ji has gone to Ajmer). It could also be read as: Guru Ji aj mar gai han (Guru Ji has died today). There was a danger that the Guru's hymns written in Lande

Mahajni might be misread and misinterpreted. He modified the existing Dev Nagari script and called it 'Gurmukhi'—meaning from the mouth of the Guru. According to Mahman Prakash the Gurmukhi script was invented by Angad at the suggestion of Guru Nanak during the founder's time.

The Guru spread the message of Guru Nanak for thirteen years and he made sure that the compositions of Guru Nanak and his own were made available to all Sikhs. Langar (free kitchen) was continued the same way as it was started by Guru Nanak. The Langar was run out of the money or food given by the followers, and supervised by Mata Kivi (wife of Guru Angad). Guru Angad did not live on the offerings of the followers. He earned his living by twisting coarse grass (munj) into strings used for making a cot.

Most of his disciples were illiterate and he used to teach them Gurmukh so that they could read the hymns of Guru Nanak. Gurudwara was used as a classroom and children and adults were taught to read and write the script. The Guru started games and sports to promote physical culture of the people. The village common was used as a sports ground and wrestling tournaments were organised to make the people health-conscious.

The Guru's programme to uplift the common people brought him in conflict with vested interest. One local ascetic called Tappa told his villagers that the drought was due to the presence of Guru Angad in Khadur. The Guru shifted to another village but the drought continued. In the end the villagers came to the Guru to save them from drought. He told them to pray to God sincerely for rainfall. After sometime, the rain fell and there was a good harvest. The villagers apologised to the Guru and brought him back to the village with great reverence. The Guru sent some devotees to preach Sikhism in neighbourhood. It is believed that Sri Chand (Guru Nanak's son) wanted to join the Guru for spreading Guru Nanak's mission, but he was told that there was no place for an ascetic like him to Nanak's teachings as his religion belonged to the householders.

Another incident in the life of Guru Angad showed his humility and tactfulness. According to Sikh tradition when Humayun was fleeing to Iran he waited upon Guru Angad at Khadur and asked him to bless him with a boon of sovereignty. The Guru kept silent and it enraged the Emperor who drew out his sword at the Guru. The Guru remarked that his sword should have been better used against his rival Sher Shah Suri rather than against an innoceent man of God who could not grant him the boon. According to Sikh tradition—Humayun's temper cooled down and he expressed regret and the Guru blessed him good luck. The Guru forgave the Emperor and gave no importance to the incident.

A local Zamindar (Goind Marwaha) requested the Guru to establish a new village on his land. The Guru agreed to establish a new village named Goindwal. At the age of 73, on one wintry night in 1552, Amardas was carrying a water-pitcher for the bath of Guru Angad, he stumbled into a pit on the way. He did not allow the water to spill, keeping it firmly on his head. Guru Angad was highly impressed by hearing the story and was so convinced by Amrdas's devotion and service that he nominated him his successor.

Amar Das, Guru (1552-1574), Third Guru

Guru Angad nominated his 73 year old disciple Amar Das as his successor. He was born on 5 May 1479, in a Bhalla Khatri family at village Basarke about 13 kms from Amritsar. His father was Tej Bhan, a local petty trader. They were all orthodox Hindus and vegetarian. At the age of 23, Amar Das married Mansa Devi, daughter of Shri Dev Chand. He had two sons Mohan and Mohri and two daughters Dani Devi and Bhani Devi.

He often went to Hardwar and Jawalamukhi on a pilgrimage, and strictly observed all the religious rites and ceremonies. He used to serve holy men. At the age of sixty Amar Das met a holy man who enquired about the name of his Guru. He answered that he had none. The holy man expressed surprise, and suggested that he must have one as early as possible. The incidence proved to be a turning point in his life and he began his search for a spiritual guide. Near his house there lived his brother Manak Chand. His son was married to Bibi Amro, daughter of Guru Angad. She used to sing Guru Angad's hymns every morning. One day he enquired whose hymns she was singing. He came to know that this was a hymn of Guru Nanak who had passed away, but his successor was Guru Angad, Bibi Amro's father. Guru Angad was only 37 years old when Amar Das became his disciple at the age of 62.

Amar Das held the office of Guru from 1552 to 1574. He moved to Goindwal situated not far away from Khadur, about 8 kilometres from Kapurthala. He did so to avoid the impending conflict with Guru Angad's sons who had not approved of their super succession. Even at Goindwal he was harassed by one of the sons named Datu. He went to Goindwal, kicked the Guru, and said that you were a water-carrier in our house and now you have become a Guru. The Guru retired from Goindwal and hid himself in a house at Basarke, his home village. Datu set himself up as the Guru. Amar Das was persuaded by Bhai Budha to return. Datu did not have much following and went back to Khadur.

The Guru wanted to meet the whole families of his Sikhs, and establish close personal bond with men, women and children. He used to meet them on Baisakhi fair (March-April) and Diwali fair (October-November) For the first time women moved freely with uncovered faces and ate in the Guru's Langar (free kitchen).

Guru Nanak had established Sangats (congregations of worshippers) at different places. The Sangats of distant places desired that they should be locally united to hold Kirtans (devotional worship). The previous Gurus moved about preaching and meeting their disciples. Guru Amr Das was old and did not like to travel much. As a visitor to Hardwar, the Guru knew that the Pandas (priests) had divided their own areas of operation. A Panda or his representative visited his devotee once a year. He divided the area inhabited by his devotees into 22 branches called Manjis or preaching assignments.

A Manji covered a certain specified area. Literally it means a cot. The Guru or local representative on a visit would sit on it (Manji). The congregation sat around on the floor. The Manji or area was in charge of a devout disciple who collected offerings for the Langar (free kitchen) as well as for the Guru's fund, and deposited in the Guru's treasury twice a year. They were to initiate people into Sikhism and carry on missionary work in their areas. The Manjis were established in Manjha, Jalandhar Doab, Kangra Hills, Kashmir Hills, Malwa and Sind.

Secondly, the Guru made the Langar (free kitchen) as part of the Sikh Gurdwaras. The institution of regular Langar where people sat in rows to take simple food without any distinction of caste or creed emphasised both equality and humility. Moreover, charity was institutionalised and became the backbone for the supply of requirements of the Langar (free kitchen)

Guruship made hereditary from Guru Amar Das

Guru Amar Das made a departure from the previous practice in appointing his successor. According to Sikh tradition the Guru was highly pleased with the single minded devotion and service of his daughter Bibi Bhani and son-in-law, Ram Das, a Sodhi Khatri of Lahore, conferred the guruship on the latter and his descendants, thereby making this office hereditary based on the principle of selection. The claims of his own sons were turned down.

It is known that the Guru trained Ram Das or popularly called Bhai Jetha (eldest child) who had been in contact with Amar Das since 1546. He found him suitable enough to wed his daughter (Bhani) to him.

Akbar and Amar Das, Guru (1574-1581), Fourth Guru

The great Emperor Akbar held the Gurus in great reverence. The Emperor visited the Guru at Goindwal and dined in Guru Ka Langar (free kitchen) The Sikhs were deeply impressed and the Emperor offered a few villages revenue-free for the support of the Langar. The Guru respectfully declined saying that the Langar depended solely on the offerings of the Sikhs. On learning that the Guru's son-in-law, Ram Das, was in search of some land, the Emperor granted a tract of land in the heart of Majha to Bibi Bhani. The Guru could not refuse a gift to his girl.

Ram Das, Guru (1574-1581), Fourth Guru

Ram Das was generally called Jetha (eldest son), and was born at Lahore on 24 September 1534. His father Hari Das a Sodhi Khatri was a trader. He was only seven when his father and mother died one after the other. His grandmother took him to her village Basarke and both of them lived there for five years. In 1546 he went to Khadur to attend Guru Angad's sermon. There he met Guru Amar Das who liked him very much. The major portion of his life was spent under the care of Guru Amar Das who taught him Panjabi and Gurbani. Amar Das took him to Goindwal—a new township where the boy earned his living by selling boiled grain. In 1552 when Amar Das became the third Guru, Ram Das served in the Langar and also did various other jobs.

One day Guru Amar Das enquired from his wife what kind of boy she desired for their daughter Bhani. Ram Das was standing there also serving the devotees. The Guru's wife pointed towards Ram Das, saying such a boy would be quite suitable. The Guru remarked that she had already found the groom and there was no need to search anywhere else. The Guru had known him since 1546 and liked him very much. In 1553 at the age of 17 he got married to Bibi Bhani, younger daughter of Guru Amar Das.

Guru Amar Das decided to set up a new town to serve as a centre for the Sikhs. He asked Ram Das to select a place.

He chose a jungle site about 40 Kms. from Goindwal. It was a common land granted by Emperor Akbar to Guru Amar Das. According to the Gazetteers of the Amritsar District in 1577, he obtained a grant of the site, together with 500 Bigahs of land, from the Emperor Akbar on payment of Rs. 700. One Bigah is equivalent to 120 feet square. The first task was the provision of water supply; so Ram Das planned the construction of a huge tank. This was constructed under the supervision of Bhai Buddha. A number of people started living around this tank. The place was known as Guru Ka Chak, Chak Guru Ram Das or Ramdaspura, later called Amritsar. Slowly a shopping centre opened there to meet the needs of the workers digging the tank. Later the shopping centre came to be known as Guru ka Bazar. Guru Ram Das started construction of another tank called Santokhsar.

As Guru Amar Das was getting very old, he decided to hold a test among his two sons-in-laws whom he thought suitable for succession. In the test Ram Das, called Jetha emerged successful and he was declared the fourth Guru in 1574 at the age of forty, and held the office for seven years only. Mohan, the elder son of Guru Amar Das deeply resented his father's decision not to give him the office of Guru. He became so much disappointed that he shut himself in a room and became a recluse. The Guru's younger son Mohri and elder son-in-law Ram, reconciled themselves.

Guru Ram Das shifted from Goindwal to Ramdaspur in 1577 to develop the new town. He persuaded many artisans, craftsmen and traders to settle in the new town. To strengthen mission work, the Guru set up a new organisation called Masand or donation collectors. The Masands carried messages of the Guru to different villages and collected donations for the development of Amritsar and local welfare projects. The Guru composed a large number of hymns for special occasions, religious ceremonies, marriage, wedding songs and songs to be sung as a prelude to marriage.

Once Sri Chand, the son of Guru Nanak, the founder of the Udasi sect, came to Goindwal to meet the Guru. The Guru warmly received him. Sri Chand asked the Guru, why he had grown a long beard. The Guru answered that it was grown to wipe the feet of holy men like you. Sri Chand was highly impressed by the Guru's sincerity and thanked him for his hospitality.

The Guru contributed a lot to Sikhism. He composed more than 800 hymns in 30 ragas. He gave the Sikhs a new town as a centre of Sikh worship, trade and education. He lay down the Sikh routine and code of conduct and paved the way for the development of his followers. He told his followers that they could please the True Guru through service and servitude. The Guru's deep humility and his spirit of service and devotion throughout his life were a great source of inspiration for his followers. He daily attended the Langar (free kitchen), and there he established perfect unity between himself and his followers.

The Guru nominated his youngest son Arjan Mal (later Guru Arjan Dev) as his successor. The Guru's eldest son Prithi Mal was very annoyed and became rude to his father (Guru Ram Das). His insulting behaviour towards the Guru and his younger brother continued. The number of followers started dwindling owing to Prithi Mal's opposition. The sad Guru breathed his last on 1 September 1581, at the age of 37. In his memory a samadhi was created at Goindwal on the bank of the river Beas.

Arjan Dev, Guru (1581-1606), Fifth Guru

Guru Arjan was the fifth Guru born at Goindwal on 15 April 1563. He was the third and the youngest son of Guru Ram Das and mother Bibi Bhani. He had two elder brothers (Pritha Mal and Maha Dev), but Guru Ram Das nominated his youngest son Arjan Mal as his successor. Arjan became Guru at the age of eighteen on 1 September 1581.

Guru Ram Das's eldest son Prithi Mal was very annoyed and became rude to his father, as he was not nominated as his successor. His insulting behaviour towards the Guru and his younger brother Arjan continued. The number of followers started dwindling owing to Prithi Mal/Pritha Mal's opposition. Guru Arjan forgave his brother and proved to be a dutiful son, conciliatory brother, and loving husband, beloved master and devoted servant of God. He was an original thinker, poet, philosopher, statesman, scholar, founder of pools and town, and the first martyr to Sikh faith.

After becoming Guru he needed money to complete the construction of both the tanks and temples left unfinished by his father. The Guru made it compulsory for every devotee to pay one-tenth of their earnings for construction and welfare projects. For collecting money he nominated some Jat Sikhs as Masands. The Masands were not paid a salary, but they retained one-third of the money and other offerings received from the Sikhs. The Masands collected offerings regularly and paid them to the Guru on Diwali and Baisakhi days. This was a great source of income for the construction of buildings and welfare programmes. The tank Amrit Sarovar (The Pool of Nectar) was finished in 1588, and Raja of Mandi (Himachal Pradesh) paid Rs. 4,000 for its construction. The Guru started construction of Hari Mandir (Golden Temple) in Amritsar and provided four doorways one on each side of the temple. It meant that God lived everywhere and was open to all the Hindus and other religions of India (Hindus, Buddhist, Muslims, Sikhs and Christians), and all the people of the world from north, south, east and west. It was a temple to sing the glory of God. It became the greatest place of pilgrimage for the devotees. The Guru started living at Amritsar and Diwali and Baisakhi celebrations became very important to every one.

Another important task, which the Guru undertook, was to consolidate and spread Sikhism by undertaking missionary tours. In 1590 he laid out another holy tank at Taran Taran about twenty kilometres from Amritsar. Taran Taran meant world's ocean, and it became another place of pilgrimage for the devotees. The popularity of Guru Arjan's missionary work attracted many devotees.

At Kartarpur, about sixty kilometres to Amritsar the Guru dug another tank called Gangasar. The township around the tank was named Kartarpur (abode of God). He built another well called Baoli at Lahore where his father was born. The Mughal army was preparing to attack the Guru when he left Amritsar and went to a village called Wadali. The drinking water was not available in the village. He dug a well there, which was called Chhehrata—the well, which worked by six Persian wheels. Later the place was called Chhehrata.

The Guru encouraged his devotees to engage in trade and commerce in addition to agriculture. Many of his devotees started trading in horses, which were bought from Central, and West Asia and sold in India. He also organised some trade in horses for himself to meet his personal expenses. The Sikhs became good horsemen and formed the nucleus of the Guru Hargobind's military power. Gradually the devotees became rich and adventurous. The Guru started living in an aristocratic style. He advocated that spiritual life and worldly living were two aspects of the same thing. He wore rich clothes, kept fine horses, some elephants and bodyguards. His devotees called him Sacha Padshah (True King).

Emperor Akbar came to see the Guru on 24 November 1598. The Guru recited a hymn of Guru Nanak in praise of God and offered him a present out of regard for his visit. He requested the Emperor to reduce the enhanced revenue on poor farmers. The Emperor reduced the revenue by one-sixth, as he was very much impressed by the warm reception given to him by the Guru. The visit raised the prestige of the Guru in the eyes of his devotees and other people. In 1605, a complaint was lodged that the Adi Granth contained some blasphemous passages to Islam. Bhai Buddha assured the Emperor that there was nothing in the Granth against Islam. The Emperor asked a Qazi and Pandit to read some passages of the Granth. The Emperor was satisfied that there was nothing against Islam and he made an offering of

51 gold coins to the Granth and awarded robes of honour to the Guru and also to the custodians of the Granth (Bhai Buddha and Bhai Gurdas).

The most valuable contribution by the Guru was the compilation of the Adi Granth or Guru Granth Sahib. The Guru laid down the exact hymns to be sung at the right time and the correct rituals to be performed by the Sikhs. This was essential as his elder brother Prithi Mal/Pritha Mal was composing his own hymns and telling the devotees that they were written by Guru Nanak and other Gurus. The Guru also wanted to collect the hymns of all the Gurus including his own in the form of a book in Gurmukhi script.

The hymns of Guru Nanak, some saints (Bhakats), Guru Angad, Amar Das and Ram Das were available in the form of Bani Pothi (Book of Hymns). This book (Bani Pothi) was arranged and written in Gurmukhi script by Guru Amar Das's grandson, Sahansar Ram, son of Mohan, in two volumes (300 leaves and 224 leaves). This also contained the hymns of Jaidev, Kabir, Ravidas, Sain and Trilochan. These two volumes were in the possession of Mohan who lived at Goindwal. He refused to give the books to anyone, but in 1603 AD he gave the two volumes to Guru Arjan. On his return he went to Khadur to meet Datu, the eldest son of Guru Angad, and collected some hymns of Guru Nanak and Guru Angad, from him. He collected some more hymns from other sources and came to Amritsar. The compiler of the hymns was Guru Arjan, but he dictated them to Bhai Gurdas who was a great scholar of Sanskrit, Hindi, Persian and Panjabi languages.

The hymns were arranged in three parts: (1) Part one consisted of morning and evening prayers—Guru Nanak's Japji and other devotional hymns. (2) The second part contained hymns arranged in thirty Ragas. (3) The third part called Bhog di Bani—includes panegyrics of the first five Gurus, and sayings of some saints and bards. The Adi Granth was completed in July 1604 and was given to Bhai Bano for getting it bound at Lahore. Bhano had the Holy Granth copied and he presented both volumes to the Guru. He put his signature on the second volume to certify its authenticity. The original Granth was installed at the Hari Mandir (Amritsar) on 16 August 1604 and Bhai Buddha was appointed as the first Granthi to recite the Granth. Now the original copy of the Adi Granth by Guru Arjan is available at the Gurdwara at Kartarpur.

The Guru's compositions in the Adi Granth include the Bara Maha, Bawan Akhri, Chaubole, Funhe, Gatha, Sukhmani Var Basant, Var Gujri, Jaisri, Var Maru and the Var Ramkali. The Granth serves as a representation of the Gurus, who are represented as one Guru or an incarnation of the Guru Nanak. The hymns of the Hindu saints usually represent Vaishnavism of Rama Nand and the Krishna cult of Surdas.

The Guru was a great saint, but still had some enemies from his own family and the Mughal Government, who were jealous of his popularity.

The Guru's elder brother Prithi Mal and his son Meharban declared themselves as Gurus. Meharban wrote a Janam Sakhi of Guru Nanak in which he glorified his father and discredited Guru Nanak. Both father and son plotted against Guru Arjan. Sulahi Khan of Batala (Mughal Officer) wanted to kill the Guru. Under severe persecution the Guru left Amritsar for Chhehrata. Chandu Shah, a revenue officer with the Mughals was annoyed with the Guru as he refused to marry his son Hargobind to the only daughter of Chandu Shah.

Emperor Jahangir and orthodox Muslims were opposed to Akbar's policy of liberality and toleration. On the death of Akbar the throne was contested between Jahangir and his son Khusarau. Jahangir succeeded to the throne and Khusrau went on the run when he met Guru Arjan at Taran Taran. The Guru welcomed Prince Khasurau and applied a saffron mark on his forehead as an honourable reception. The Prince requested some financial help and the Guru gave him a few thousand rupees. Khusrau was captured on 26

April 1606 and produced before Jahangir partially blinded. The Emperor summoned the Guru to Lahore and asked him why he had helped the Prince with money and also applied the saffron mark on his forehead for victory. The Guru replied that he gave him some money for his journey and the saffron mark was a traditional Hindu welcome to the Prince. Jahangir did not feel satisfied with the reply. He wanted to put him to death, but on the request of a Muslim holy man (Mia Mir), he commuted it by a fine of two lakhs of rupees, and ordered him to delete some verses from the holy Granth Sahib. The Guru replied that whatever he had was for the poor, and he would not pay a single penny as a fine. The Guru believed that the fine was imposed on criminals and wicked people, but not on holy people and priests. The Guru refused to pay the fine, as he was not guilty of any crime and also refused to delete any hymns from the Granth, as there was nothing against Islam. The devotees wanted to raise two lakhs rupees to pay the fine, but the Guru issued instructions not to do so. The Guru's property was confiscated, and he was sent to prison in Lahore Fort and tortured. The property of the Guru could not fetch two lakh rupees, and the balance of the money was demanded from his son Hargobind. He was sent to Gwalior prison for twelve years for the non-payment of the fine.

Before execution Guru Arjan was given permission to bathe in the river Ravi as he did not want to die unclean. On 30 May 1606 the Guru died while bathing and his body was washed away by the strong currents of the river. His samadhi (tomb) was later erected at the site on the bank of river Ravi opposite to the Fort of Lahore.

Hargobind, Guru (1606-1644), Sixth Guru

Guru Hargobind was the only child of Guru Arjan Dev and Mata Ganga born on 14 June 1595 in the village of Wadali, near Amritsar. There is a legend that he was born with the blessing of Bhai Buddha. He was nominated by Guru Arjan as the sixth Guru at the age of eleven. He wore two swords of Piri and Miri (spiritual power and secular sovereignty).

The Guru became a father of six children from three wives. Gurditta, Ami Rai, and daughter Viro were born to Mata Damodri, Suraj Mal and Atal Rai from Mata Mahadevi and Tegh Bahadur from Mata Nanaki.

He armed and trained his followers to become saint soldiers. When he became the fifth Guru he had only fifty-two soldiers. He increased them to three hundred horsemen, seven hundred horses, sixty gunners and five hundred infantry men. All his followers believed that by fighting in the cause of Dharma (righteousness) they would attain salvation. He built a fortress at Amritsar called Lohgarh, had his own flag and a big drum which was beaten at sunrise and sunset.

Hargobind combined the qualities of a warrior, a saint and a sportsman. He was compelled by the Muslim rulers to resort to arms, and was the first Guru to organise a military system by arming his followers, and teaching them the art of war. All the previous Gurus were vegetarians and they forbade animal food. He believed that there was no harm in eating meat if you have to fight the enemy while living in jungles. He built the town of Hargobindpur on the banks of the river Beas, to serve, in case of an emergency, as a place of retreat. He maintained a large establishment with offerings from his followers throughout the country.

The first phase of his life was devoted to building up the morale of his followers. His mission was to make the Sikh community self-reliant, brave and secular. He trained his followers in martial arts, and horsemanship. The court musicians sang old Hindu heroic poems to inspire the Sikhs to emulate the heroic deeds of well-known Rajput warriors. Wrestling matches, and swordsmanship became very popular during his time. The character of his followers was moulded for self-defence and armed opposition to injustice and oppression. The Guru maintained a royal court and had 52 guards.

In front of the Hari Mandar he constructed the Akal Takht (God's throne) in 1606, and sat there like a prince on a raised platform twelve feet high. Hari Mandar was a seat of his spiritual authority and the Akal Takht was the seat of his temporal authority. In the Akal Takht he administered justice, accepted gifts of arms, horses, money and awarded honours and punishments. He trained his soldiers and narrated stories of Rajput chivalry that fought against the Muslims. He continued preaching and spreading his faith despite unfavourable political situation in Panjab. The Guru's warlike talent led him to enter the service of Jahangir as a military leader, and he even accompanied the emperor Jehangir to his visit to Kashmir. During the emperor's residence at Lahore he became a great friend of his son Dara Shekoh. He also used to go to Kashmir with Dara Shekoh on pleasure trips. (Dabistan Mazhab of Mohsin Fani p.274).

The emperor Jahangir received a lot of reports that Guru Hargobind was raising a revolt against him. The Guru fell into the estimation of the Emperor through appropriating to his own use the pay of the contingent, and by failing to pay the balance of the heavy fine that had been imposed upon his father Guru Arjan Dev (fifth Guru). The emperor was annoyed and ordered the Guru to pay the balance of the fine of two lakh rupees imposed upon Guru Arjan Dev. Guru Hargobind refused to pay the fine. Jahangir wrote in his diary that the Guru was extremely arrogant and therefore he sentenced him to imprisonment in Gwalior prison. In Gwalior prison all the prisoners were usually allowed to keep their wives provided they observed the same rules as prisoners. The Guru was set free after twelve years on the recommendation of Mian Mir, a Muslim saint. But the Guru would accept the release only on the condition that his fellow prisoners were also released with him. The emperor agreed and 52 princes holding on to the Guru's big robe came out of the prison. Due to this the Guru earned the title of Bandichar (liberator of the bonded).

Mian Mir (Muslim Saint) however interceded with Jahangir at Delhi and not only obtained his release but reconciled him to this emperor whom he accompanied on his tour in Rajputana and whom he even employed to subdue the rebellious chief of Nallagarh. This account is reconcilable with Dabistan Mazhab of Mohsin Fani (p.274) which represents Guru Hargobind as entering Jahangir's service and continuing to serve Shah Jahan: yet the latter emperor sent troops against him and they drove him out of Ramdaspur (Amritsar) and plundered his lands there.

The Guru had some enemies: Prithi Mal (eldest brother of his father) was his bitter enemy as he was not chosen by his father (the fourth Guru) to become the Guru. Prithi Mal continuously complained against the Guru to the Mughal officers of the province as well as directly to the Emperor. Prithi Mal called himself the sixth Guru and his son Meharban called himself the seventh Guru. Chandu Shah was another enemy of the Guru as he wanted to marry his daughter to the Guru, but he refused to marry her. Murtga Khan (Governor of Panjab) was deadly foe of the Sikhs.

Guru Hargobind spent the last nine years of his life at Kiratpur attending congregational prayers and advising his followers. The Guru's activities were not appreciated by some Hindus. Many Sikhs complained that the Guru had not added a verse to the Holy Granth and led a roving life. Former Gurus sat on a cot and gave consolation to their followers, but Guru Hargobind kept dogs and spent his time hunting. The previous Gurus composed hymns and the followers listened to them and sang their hymns, but Guru Hargobind neither composed, nor listened, nor sang. Bhai Gurdas and some other Sikhs thought that his struggle against the mighty Mughals was useless. Inspite of some victories of the Guru against the Mughals he was driven away and was forced to seek refuge in the hilly region at Kiratpur.

Whatever the complaints were against the Guru, it must be admitted that he was the first Guru who resorted to arms in order to redress the grievances of the community. He believed that fighting against the wrongs was the right Dharma of the religion. He combined in himself, spiritual and political/military leadership.

Jahangir died in 1628 and his successor Shah Jahan was hostile to the Guru. He sent a force of about 7000 troops under Mukhlis Khan to teach a lesson to the Sikhs. Amritsar was plundered but when the Mughal commander was killed and Mughal forces retreated. The Guru shifted to Kartarpur. The second battle took place in 1631 at Lahira. Both sides suffered heavy losses and the Mughal commander was killed. The third battle took place in 1634 and the Mughal commanders Painde Khan and Kale Khan were killed in the battle of Kartarpur. The Guru soon became friendly with the emperor and peace was restored between 1635-1644.

The Guru devoted himself to missionary work and Baba Siri Chand a follower of Udasi sect was sent to preach Sikhism. Bidichand was sent to Bengal for missionary work, while Bhai Gurdas was entrusted with theological studies.

The Guru was very well versed in politics as he accepted high office under Jahangir and Shah Jahan. He gave lesson of holy war (dharam yudh) to his followers and considered it improper to adopt a submissive role to the Mughals. His achievements included:

1. Promotion of martial arts and war strategy to make the Sikhs face the challenge of injustice and tyranny.
2. He built Sikh temples and sent missionaries to preach Sikhism.
3. Built the Akal Takht to discuss war and peace and secular matters.
4. Built a new township called Kiratpur, which later became a centre of trade.

Guru Har Gobind appointed his grandson, Har Rai as his successor before his death on 3 March 1644.

On his death at Kiratpur in 1645 his grandson Har Rai succeeded him. Har Rai was the son of Gurditta from his first wife. Gurditta was the eldest son of Guru Har Gobind from his first wife. He became an Udasi, and this disqualified him from the office of Guru. Baba Gurditta married a second wife much against the wishes of his father, and Ram Rai was his son by that wife. We do not know why Ram Rai was not allowed to become Guru. According to Sikh accounts he had misquoted a verse of Guru Nanak

Har Rai, Guru (1644-1661), Seventh Guru

Har Rai was born on 30 January 1630 to father Gurditta and mother Nihalo Devi. He became the seventh Guru at the age of fourteen. The Guru was of a very kind and peaceful nature, but he had to maintain an army of 2,200 soldiers for the protection of his devotees. The army was raised by his grandfather to defend himself from the Mughals.

Guru Hargobind became a father of six children from three wives. Gurditta, Ami Rai, and daughter Viro were born to Mata Damodri, Suraj Mal and Atal Rai from Mata Mahadevi and Tegh Bahadur from Mata Nanaki. He did not find any one of them fit for the Guruship. The Guru's eldest son Gurditta had died in 1638, leaving behind two sons Dhir Mal and Har Rai. Dhir Mal wanted to succeed as the Guru, but the Guru nominated his fourteen years old younger brother, Har Rai, as the Guru. It was mentioned in Ramjas Diwan's Tarikh Ahluwalia. p.57 that Dhir Mal got very annoyed and he mixed poison in the evening meal of the Guru and went to Kartarpur with the original copy of the Adi Granth. The Guru died and on his funeral pyre two of his servants jumped and died with him.

Mughal army was trying to attack Raja Tara Chand Kahlur near the place where the Guru was staying. The Guru's elder brother had given himself the title of the seventh Guru at Kartarpur. Prthi Mal's son Meharban had also occupied Hari Mandar at Amritsar and declared himself the Seventh Guru. For these reasons the Guru's mother became adviser to his minor son and took him to Nahan in the country of Raja Karam Prakash near Sarhind. Guru Har Rai lived at Nahan for twelve years, though he often visited Kiratarpur. He took some missionary tours to consolidate his followers.

Prince Dara Shikoh, the eldest son of Shah Jahan, met the fifteen years old Guru Har Rai, as he was in the habit of meeting holy men. Shah Jahan fell ill in September 1657 and a war of succession started between his sons. Aurangzeb defeated Dara Shikoh and while on the run he met Guru Har Rai near Rupar. Aurangzeb became the Emperor in 1658 after killing his brothers. He was unhappy at the growing popularity of the Guru and summoned him to his court to answer charges (a) why he rendered help to his brother Dara Shikoh and (b) why there was an insulting verse in the Holy Granth against Islam. The Guru sent his fourteen-year-old son Ram Rai in September 1661 to answer the Emperor. He assured the Emperor that his father did not render any help to his brother Dara Shikoh.

He was asked to explain why the following verse in the Guru Granth Sahib abused the Muslims:

Matti Musalman ki pere pai kumhar— Ghar bhande ittan kian jalati karew pukar.

(After the death the ashes or dust of a Muslim is kneaded by a potter into a dough, and he converts it into pots and bricks—why worry as the dust or ashes of Hindus and Muslims will become one after death, and will burn together to become pots or bricks.) Guru Nanak composed this hymn to cite that cremation and burial were the same as we (Hindu and Muslims) are from the same dust and will merge into the same dust of our country after death.

In order to please the Emperor, Ram Rai replied that Nanak's actual word was Beiman or faithless and not Musalman which appeared in the text by the mistake of the scribe. It pleased the Emperor but his father Guru Har Rai was very furious and he declared Ram Rai as unfit for Guruship and excluded him from the succession. Before his death he nominated his younger son Har Krishan to be his successor and he became the Guru on 6 October 1661. It is believed that Aurangzeb put pressure on Guru Har Rai to change his verdict in favour of Ram Rai for which he did not agree. The Emperor harassed the Guru too much and due to that he died at the age of thirty-two on 6 October 1661.

The most important contribution of Guru Har Rai was the establishment of a health clinic of herbal medicines at Kiratpur. Once Dara Shikoh, son of Emperor Shah Jahan, fell ill and the required herbal medicine, which was sent to Shah Jahan from his clinic for the treatment of Dara Shikoh. He continued the tradition of Langar (free kitchen). During the famine of 1641-1649 many people were fed from his free kitchen. He was a compassionate man who raised and blessed many people, but two orphans (Phul and Sandli) are mentioned particularly in the history books. Later they became the originators of Phulkian Rajas who ruled the Patiala State.

Har Krishan, Guru (1661-1664), Eighth Guru

He was the youngest son of Guru Har Rai, born on 7 July 1656. Guru Har Rai nominated him to be his successor. Har Krishan became the Guru on 6 October 1661 at the age of five. He was known as the Child Saint. His elder brother Ram Rai claimed Guruship but he had been declared unfit for it because he had lied to the Emperor about a verse in the Guru Granth Sahib.

Ram Rai was very angry about the choice of Guruship by his father. Immediately after his father's death he declared himself as the Guru in Delhi. He started appointing his own Masand's (revenue collectors) for collecting donations. He complained to Emperor Aurangzeb that his father disowned him for his loyalty to him. The Emperor supported Ram Rai for Guruship and summoned the child Guru to Delhi to justify his claim for Guruship. Har Krishan came to Delhi and stayed in the house of Raja Jai Singh of Jaipur in the suburbs of Delhi. Within a few days the Guru had an attack of smallpox with high fever and became very ill. It is believed that before his death his followers placed a coconut and five pice (pennies) before him and asked him to name his successor. It is known that he uttered the word Baba Bakala, meaning that the next Guru should be Baba (grandfather) at a place called Bakala. Tegh Bahadur was living at Bakala and he was the son of Guru Hargobind (6th Guru). Guru Har Gobind (6th Guru) had not considered him for Guruship, as he was a recluse. The child Guru died at the age of eight on 30 March 1664. He was cremated on the bank of river Yamuna where Gurdwara Bala Sahib was built. A big Gurdwara called Bangla Sahib was later built where the Guru stayed in Delhi.

Tegh Bahadur, Guru (1621-1675) Ninth Guru

He was born on 1 April1621 to Guru Hargobind and Mata Nanaki, Tegh Bahadur, whose original name was Tyag Mal, spent is childhood at Amritsar. His life may be divided into three periods: 1621-1644, 1644-1664, and 1664-1675. In his early years he learnt Gurmukhi, Hindi, Sanskrit and Hindu religious philosophy from Bhai Gurdas, and archery and horsemanship from Bhai Buddha, while his father taught him swordsmanship. At the age of thirteen he distinguished himself in the battle of Kartarpur and it is said that he was renamed Tegh Bahadur (warrior of swordmanship) in place of Tyag Mal (man of renunciation). He married Mata Gujari at Kartarpur in 1632, when his father nominated his grandson Har Rai as his successor in 1644. At that time Tegh Bahadur moved with his wife to the village of Bakala.

The second period of his life from 1644 to 1664 was mainly a period of meditation. He also went on preaching tours from 1657 to Uttar Pradesh, Bihar and Bengal.The Guru left his wife at Patna as she was pregnant. He received the news of the birth of a son on 18 December 1661. Before Guru Harkrishan died in Delhi, he indicated that his successor would be Baba Bakala and Makhan Shah Labana declared Tegh Bahadur as the ninth Guru in August 1664.

The last period of eleven years (1664-1675) was one of Guru Tegh Bahadur's pontification. He started a new township on land purchased from Rani Champa of Bilaspur in June 1665. This came to be known as Anandpur (the city of joy). A few months later he began the second preaching tour of U.P. and Bengal. He was accompanied by his family and close relatives. He consolidated the Sangats of Bihar under the supervision of his devotee, Dayaldas.

During his tour of Assam, the Guru negotiated a treaty of peace between Raja Ram Singh (a deputy of the Mughal emperor), and the local king, King Ahom. In 1669, Emperor Aurangzeb ordered the destruction of Hindu temples and schools. During his travels, the Guru encouraged the people to stand up for their rights and protest against injustice. The Guru returned to Anandpur in 1670 and rejoined his family. He undertook a tour of Patiala region and met his Muslim admirer Saif Khan at Saifabad (now called Bahadur Garh). He also visited Damdama Sahib where he got a tank dug for the supply of water to the local residents. The Guru rewarded the local people who supported the welfare projects.

At that time Emperor Aurangzeb intensified his policy of persecution of Hindus and the use of force for conversion of Hindus to Islam in Panjab and Kashmir. He asked the local Governor of Kashmir to put pressure on the Hindu Pandits to embrace Islam. The Pandits came to Anandpur to seek the Aid of the Guru Tegh Bahadur. So Guru Tegh Bahadur decided to stand up for the right of freedom of worship and told the Pandits of Kashmir that he was ready to sacrifice his life to protect the Hindus from mass conversion. When Aurangzen learnt this, he ordered the arrest of the Guru, whom he called the Pir of Hindus. The Guru nominated his son (Gobind Rai/later Gobind Singh) as his successor Guru and proceeded towards Delhi. In Delhi he was imprisoned with his devotees and tortured. He was asked to become a Muslim. His three devoted followers, who refused to become Muslims were tortured to death in his presence. On 11

November 1675, the Guru was beheaded, and his head fell at some distance and was picked up by Bhai Jetha and taken to Anandpur.Bhai Lakhi Shahi carried the body of the Guru in a Bullock cart to his house. Fearing punishment from the Emperor, he set his own house, containing the body on fire for cremation. At this spot stands Gurdwara Rakabganj in New Delhi. Reverentially the Guru is called (Hind the Chadar) the saviour of the honour of India. His sacrifice symbolised courage and determination in the cause of religious freedom, as also the struggle for preservation of human values and righteousness.

The Guru was a remarkable poet and musicologist. He composed his hymns in Hindi in 15 classical ragas. The hymns are included in the Adi Granth by his son (Guru Gobind Singh). They embody a message of freedom, courage and compassion (fear not and frighten not). They enshrine his vision of the God-man (Gurmukh).

The Guru had a versatile personality—a warrior, a family man with social commitments, a preacher of great understanding and vision. His martyrdom broke the myth of Aurangzeb's religiosity. The emperor realised his mistake later before his death.

The achievements of the Guru are remarkable: first, he founded the city of Anandpur and started projects of welfare all over northern India. Secondly he inspired his devotees with courage and fearlessness, he symbolised the triumph of good over evil and espoused the ultimate sovereignty of virtue, truth, justice and freedom. Thirdly, his martyrdom inspired many Sikhs to lay down their lives for noble cause and moral values.

Gobind Singh (1666-1708), Tenth Guru

Known as: (Gobind Das/Gobind Rai, Guru from 1666-1699);

Known as: Gobind Singh Guru (from 30 March 1699-1708 after the Pahul ceremony)

The Guru was born on 22 December 1666 and his father (9th Guru Tegh Bahadur) named him Gobind Das. His mother Mata Gujri was living at that time in Patna (Bihar), while his father had gone on a missionary tour of East Bengal. He spent his early years in Patna and learnt Sanskrit, Hindi, Gurmukhi, Persian, Arabic and Arithmetic. He also learnt the use of arms from early childhood. His parents returned to Anandpur in 1670It was in 1675 when the Kashmiri Pandits came to Guru Tegh Bahadur to request him to intercede with the Mughal emperor to stop forcible conversion to Islam. Gobind Das/Gobind Rai advised his father to save them with the sacrifice of his life. After his father's martyrdom, he became the 10th Guru at the age of nine in 1675. In those days the emperor levied an excessive tribute on the hill chiefs, but they refused to pay and requested Guru Gobind Singh to help them. He joined them to resist the attack by the Mughal army and became victorious.

From the age of nine to thirty-nine, the Guru fought about twenty battles, nine before the creation of the Khalsa and eleven afterwards. The Guru was only sixteen years old when he became very popular at Anandpur in the state of Kahlur. The Raja of Kahlur could not tolerate his popularity and sovereignty within his state. Therefore the Raja attacked him, but got defeated by the Guru. The Guru's army consisted of Hindus and Muslims. In 1685 the Guru shifted to Paonta, about 50 kms from Dehradun). There he organised his army and offered patronage to poets. At Anandpur he composed Japu, Akal Utsat and translated from Sanskrit into Brajbhasha an episode of Markendaya Puran (known as Chandi ki Var). It celebrates goddess Durga's victories over the Asuras (demons), fought in the cause of freedom, righteousness and justice. He wrote these poems to inspire his soldiers for the coming struggle with tyrannical princes. He also completed Krishna Avtar in July 1688. In Krishna Avtar the Guru says: that no one can have sovereignty as a gift from another, and it is to be achieved through one's own strength.

He laid down the principles of Dharam Yudh (war for righteousness and justice), and organised mock battles for training his followers in the strategy of war. His devotees brought him horses, swords and many precious gifts. The prince of Assam presented him with many weapons and a performing elephant. The Guru got a large drum made and called it Ranjit Nagara (the drum of victory).

The notable scholars/poets at the Guru's court were Hans Ram, Chandan and Sainapat. They translated into Hindi, stories of heroism from the Ramayana, Mahabharata and Puranas. From 1669 to 1679 Aurangzeb ordered that all temples and schools of Hindus should be demolished, and Hindus were asked to pay Jazia (tax being non-Muslim) from 2 April 1679. All the state officials were ordered to embrace Islam, and conversion of Hindus to Islam was in full swing. From Bombay to Madras the Marathas plundered the territory mercilessly. In Panjab the Guru was determined to exterminate the religious oppression of the emperor Aruangzeb. Like Shiva Ji Marhatta (Maharashtra) he fought against the cruel Emperor Aurangzeb and his army and not against Islam. The Guru tried to create national awakening in the Panjab as it had been done in Maharashtra by Shivaji. In Bachitra Natak, the Guru prays to Lord Shiva to give him strength to fight against cruelty and injustice.

In the hill areas the mother goddess was the most common object of veneration and worship for the people. According to the Guru, the Goddess symbolised divine power with a holy sword in hand and riding a lion. In Chandi Charitra the Guru says that the Goddess was the war hero and she would help us to get rid of the Mughal tyrant and their evil. He was a brave warrior with limitless energy, high-minded, superhuman will power, marvellous intellect, and was the most prominent and the most amiable and interesting of all the leaders of that time. He is said to have married thrice. Three sons were born from his wife Jito and one from his wife Sundari. The third wife, Sahib Devi was married in 1700 on the assurance that she would remain a virgin all her life.

Therefore she was declared the mother of Khalsa.

The movement called Khalsa (pure) was the brainchild of the Guru and it transformed the timid people into a strong nation. The Guru stood for secularism, democracy, and national unity in the Indian people regardless of caste or colour. He believed in the equality of men and women and the dignity of labour. To fulfil his wishes he instituted a new ceremony of baptism. This was given religious sanction on the Hindu Baisakhi festival at Anandpur in 1699 when he baptised five persons of different castes into a new fraternity of Khalsa (pure). He asked his followers to join and shed all the superstitions of caste, birth and base all their belief in One God (Ik Omkar).

The last phase of his life (1699-1708) was partly spent in waging holy wars against the tyrannical chiefs, specially the Moghul emperor. The Mughal army surrounded the Guru's fort at Anandpur. Fearing starvation, some forty Sikhs left the Guru, and soon after the Guru agreed to leave the fort on the guarantee of safe conduct by the Mighal commander. On a wintry night the Guru marched towards Chamkur and disguised as a holy man (Uch ka Pir) passed safely through enemy territory. Later he was followed by the Mughal troops near Muktsar. The forty Sikhs, who had earlier deserted, returned to and fight for the Guru, but they all died fighting the Mughal forces. The Guru saw from a mound their gallant fight against thousands of the enemy forces, and reached the spot where Bhai Mahan Singh was lying fatally wounded, but alive to see the Guru tearing the letter of disclaimer which those Sikhs had earlier signed against him.

In the meantime the Guru wrote a poetic letter entitled Zafarnama to Emperor Aurangzeb. The Emperor was moved by the Guru's epistle, and was overcome by remorse, but died before the Guru could meet him. Nawab Nazir Khan of Sarhind sent his trusted assassins to murder the Guru at Nander. They pretended to be his devotees and one night entered his tent stealthily and fatally stabbed him. Emperor Bahadur Shah sent his surgeon to dress the Guru's wounds, but unfortunately the Guru's condition worsened. The Guru, knowing his end was approaching, called a special congregation on 7 October 1708. He announced the end of personal Guruship and passed on the perpetual Guruship to the Guru Granth Sahib. The place where the Guru was cremated is called Takht Sri Hazur Sahib at Nander in the state of Maharashtra.

The main achievements of the Guru were: (1) The creation of Khalsa brotherhood through the ceremony of Pahul. (2) Literary works which were later compiled as the Dasam Granth by Bhai Mani Singh. (3) Waging of righteous war called Dharam Yudh against tyrannical rulers. (4) Tradition to pass resolutions (Gurmattas) binding on all Sikhs. (5) Sacrifice of himself and his four sons for the protection of the Sikh community. (6) Passing on the succession of Guruship to the Guru Granth Sahib.

Sikhism—Chronological tables/ movement
Sikh Gurus and contemporary Mughal Emperors

Guru's name	Birth	Installation as Guru	Death	Mughals
1. Guru Nanak	15.4.1469		22.9.1539	Lodi/Babar
2. Guru Angad	31.3.1504	14.6.1539	29.3.1552	Humayun
3. Guru Amar Das	5.5.1479	29.3.1552	1.9.1574	Akbar
4. Guru Ram Das	24.9.1534	1.9.1574	1.9.1581	Akbar
5. Guru Arjan	5.4.1563	1.9.1581	30.5.1606	Jahangir
6. Guru Hargobind	14.6.1595	25.5.1606	3.3.1644	Shahjahan
7. Guru Har Rai	26.2.1630	8.3.1644	6.10.1661	Shahjahan
8. Guru Har Krishan	7.7.1656	7.10.1661	30.3.1664	Aurangzeb
9. Guru Tegh Bahaduer	1.4.1621	20.3.1665	11.11.1675	Aurangzeb
10. Guru Gobind Singh	22.12.1666	1.11.1675	7.10.1708	Bahadur Shah

Guru Granth Sahib Installation

Two celebrations are held: the first installation of the Sikh scripture in the Golden Temple (held in August 1604). The second is the installation of Guru Granth Sahib as the permanent Guru by Guru Gobind Singh (at Nander in October 1708). It is called Guru Granth Guryal Gurparb.

Sikh Power from Banda Bahadur to Mahan Singh 1708-1712. Banda Bahadur succeeds Guru Gobind Singh as leader of the Sikhs in 1708 during the reign of Bahadur Shah (1707-1712). Banda Bahadur conquered many cities in Panjab and became ruler of some parts of Panjab. Banda was captured and killed by Abdur Samad.

Nadir Shaha invaded Panjab in 1739, and Ahmad Shah invaded Panjab eight times (1747-1767).

The Sikhs under Jassa Singh occupy Lahore in 1758. And 1764.

Death of Ahmad Shah in 1767 (during the invasion of Panjab).

Bhangi and Sukarchakia misls take part in the Kashmir rebellion. Death of Charat Singh in 1773 and Mahan Singh married Raj Kaur.

Ranjit Singh and his reign in Panjab lasted from 1792 to 1839.

After his death there were two Sikh wars with the British and finally the British defeated the Sikhs and became rulers of the Panjab as well in March 1849.

1873 to	1992
1873	First Singh Sabha founded in Amritsar
1879	Another Singh Sabha founded in Lahore
1898	Ham Hindu nahin hain by Kahan Singh of Nabha
1902	Chief Khalsa Diwan established and Anand Marriage Act was passed
1913	Rakabganj Gurdwara campaign
1919	Central Sikh League was founded
1920-25	Gurdwara Reform Movement

1925 Gurdwara Act was passed
1947 15 August. Independence of India and partition.
1966 Panjabi state on the basis of mother tongue.

1984, 4 June

Bhindrawala and many of his followers were hiding in the Golden Temple. Jarnail Singh Bhindranwala preached against Hindus and Mrs. Gandhi's government. On 3 June 1984 the Indian army surrounded the Golden Temple and 35 other Gurdwaras where the extremist were hiding. Bhindrawala and most of his followers were killed in the Army operation named 'Operation Blue Star' which lasted for five days.

1984, 31 October

Mrs. Indra Gandhi (Prime Minister of India) was assassinated by her Sikh guards. Many followers of Mrs. Gandhi killed many innocent Sikhs in Delhi

Rajiv Gandhi succeeded his mother as Prime Minister.

1985, 24 July

The Panjab Accord was an agreement between Rajiv Gandhi, Prime Minister of India, and Sant Harchand Singh Longowal, the then leader of the moderate group in the Akali Dal in the Panjab.

1985, 20 August

The extremist Sikhs killed Sant Harchand Singh Longowal, the then leader of the moderate group in the Akali Dal in the Panjab.

1985-92

Disturbances in the Panjab. Many extremist Sikhs and innocent people were killed. In 1992 peace returned to the Panjab.

2

Traditions (Oral Transmission from Generation to Generation)

Nitnem (daily rule or routine of daily prayers)

It means recitation of certain Banis (hymns of Gurus and Bhagats) everyday by Sikhs and by the Khalsa. It is necessary for every Sikh to recite at least the following five Banis every day:

1. Japji of Guru Nanak, comprising the main peinciples of Sikh spiritualism, ethics and divinity. (2) Jap of Guru Gobind Singh, giving the attributes of God; personal and impersonal. (3) Swayas of Guru Gobind Singh, 10 hymns—including the transitories of material enjoyments and emphasizing the brevity of human life. (4) Rahiras—the prayers for the evening. (5) Kirtan Sohaila—praise of the Divine, five hymns to be recited at bedtime.

The first one is Japji of Guru Nanak. The second and third are Jap Sahib and Mukh Vak Savayyas by Guru Gobind Singh. But there are some more prayers which are recited by devotees as a part of Nitnem (daily prayers). The Anand Sahib composed by Guru Amar Das. Evening prayers also include (Shalok Mohalla 1, Sodar Mohalla 1, Asa Mohalla 1,

Rag Gujri Mohalla 4 and 5, Rag Asa Mohalla 4) and Ardas.

Japji—introductory verse

Om sat nam karta purakhu, nirbhu, akalmurti, ajuni saibham gurprasad.

The sign Om is read Ikokar, that is, ik, one plus Om (the sacred and mystic sound which the Hindus use in worship and consider to be significant of the Trimurti, that is, Brahma, Vishnu and Mahesh plus kar (syllable used in Sanskrit and Hindi to denote sound. Granthis say that ik is prefixed to show the unity of God.

Sat is for atya (Sanskrit); Hindi Sach (true and real)
Nam/Namu (name—God is called Sat Nam)
The meaning of the each word will be clear if we translate the verse as follows:
The True Name, Creator, mighty, fearless, devoid of enmity, timeless form, not liable to transmigration, self-existent, beneficient guide.

The Japji of Guru Nanak. In the morning a Sikh should get up early in the morning and bathe. He should then repeat Guru Nank's Japji, Guru Gobind Singh's Jap, and the Ten Swayyas.The Japji was composed and written by the Guru about 1520 in his old age at Kartarpur. It consists of two Shalokas, one at the beginning and the other at the end, and thirty-eight stanzas (Pauris). It is considered by the Sikhs a key to their sacred volume and an epitome of its doctrines. Every Sikh must know it by heart and is silently repeated by them every morning.

The poem starts with that there is one God whose name is true, the Creator, devoid of fear and enmity, immortal, unborn, self-existent. He says that creation, protection and dissolution represent only one Supreme Being. God uttered one word and the whole universe came into being at once. The Guru does not believe in the theory of evolution.

By thinking I cannot obtain a conception of Him, even though I think of Him hundreds of thousands of times. By His order bodies are produced: His order cannot be described, True is the Lord, true is His name; it is uttered with endless love. God is formless. He is spirit. The Guru is Shiva; the Guru is Vishnu and Brahma; the Guru is Parbati, Lakshmi, and Saraswati. Under the Guru's instruction God's word is heard; under the Guru's instruction man learns that God is everywhere contained. In stanza 34 the guru says:

God created nights, seasons, lunar days, and weekdays, wind, water, fire, and the nether regions.
In the midst of these He established the earth as a temple.
In it He placed living beings of different habits and kinds.
Their names are various and endless, and they are judged according to their deeds.
True is God and true is His court. The bad and the good shall there be distinguished.
Nanak, on arrival there, this shall be seen.
Guru Nanak lays down five stages of spiritual progress:

(a) In Dharam Khand the devotee realises that God is the creator of all things; (b) in Gian Khand the devotee gains wider knowledge and realises that God is creator, preserver and destroyer of everything; (c) in Sharam Khand a devotee realises the meaning of action and effort; (d) Karma Khand lays emphasis on good deeds; (e) Sach Khand is the realm of truth where devotee united with God and loses its individuality.

In stanza thirty-eight the Guru says in order to attain union with God, a person should follow eight stages like the minting of a gold coin:

Make continence thy furnace, resignation thy goldsmith, understanding thine anvil, Divine knowledge thy tools, the fear of God thy bellows, austerities thy fire, Divine love thy crucible, and melt God's name therein.

In such a true mint the Word shall be coined. This is the practice of those on whom God looked with an eye of favour. Nanak, the Kind One by a glance maketh them happy.

In Japji the Guru describes Almighty as one God. Complete surrender to the Almighty in thought, word and deed, and repetition of His Name wholeheartedly attain the goal of life.

Jap Sahib of Guru Gobind Singh

It is the supplement or complement of the Japji of Guru Nanak, a prayer to be read or repeated in the morning, as it continues to be by pious Sikhs. The Jap is a morning prayer of the Khalsa and Japji of Guru Nanak is a morning prayer for all the Sikhs (Sahajdaris and Khalsa). It comprises 198 distchs (verses), and occupies about seven pages, the termination of a verse and the end of a line not being the same. The Guru gives about 950 names of God in the Jap Sahib. It was perhaps the first composition written about 1684. It starts like this:

The One Aum/Om—is formless, colourless, casteless, has power beyond measure, you are the ruler of everyone, supreme sovereign of three worlds, you are the beginning and the end and you are everywhere and powerful and light and creation of the world.

God is the Supreme Power. He is most beautiful, bountiful, unborn, changeless and merciful, wielder of arms and present everywhere. The language is Hindi and Sanskrit and also includes a few Arabic words.

Swayyas/Sri Mukh Vak Swayyas

The Ten Swayyas should be daily recited after Japji and Jap Sahib. Swayyas start like this: I have found in vain men who follow pure reason, saints, yogis and wise men, but never found any one following the Lord of Life, and without the love and grace of God their devotion is worthless.

Guru dwells on the worship of formless God The verses are recited during the preparation of Amrit to be administered at baptism. Sri Mukh Vak Swayyas of voice of the Guru in 32 verses were composed by the Guru as a sermon on divinity. They occupy about three-and-a-half pages.

Sodar Rah Ras

It is sung at sung at sunset. It means the path of truth. It says that pleasures seduces mind from the God. God is the master, Lord and Creator. It is the evening prayer of the Sikhs. It occupies about three and a half pages, and it was composed by Guru Nanak, but has additions by Guru Ram Das and Guru Arjan.

Kirtan Sohela

This is a bedtime prayer of the Sikhs. It is a collection of five hymns in different ragas to be found on pages 12 and 13 of Guru Granth Sahib. This is comparatively short collection, and in the first hymn, death is compared to the farewell of a bride to her parents while moving to her husband's home. The call of death is symbolic of a spiritual wedding of the individual soul to the Supreme Soul. This is the time for the remembrance of the Holy Name.

In the second hymn the unity and diversity of god is explained through the metaphor of cycles of seasons and day and night. The sun is one, but it gives rise to different kinds of weather. Similarly behind every religion is the concept of the Supreme Being (The Almighty).

In the third hymn in Arti (adoration or prayer) form the Guru describes the worship and glorification of god by forces of nature in different ways.

In the fourth hymn it is mentioned that the devotee must humble himself before saintly people in order to win their grace and so obtain a place in god's court.

In the fifth and final hymn is a plea for spiritual effort in this short life so as to reach the goal of blissful union with god, through the company of holy people.

Sukhmani Sahib

It means the psalm of peace (peace of mind) or Jewel of bliss. Sukhmani commands a great popularity, but it is not a part of the regular daily prayers. Many Sikhs include it in their morning prayers. Many Hindus also recite it regularly. It is the most popular composition of Guru Arjan in Rag Gauri. It is said that he wrote for a devotee who was suffering from a great physical pain and mental anguish. When he listened to it he was restored to calm and health.

Sukhmani has structural unity. There are 24 cantos (parts), each containing 8 stanzas of five couplets each. It has 24 staves (shaloka), each sums up the idea of a canto (part). The main ideas of this composition are: the benefits of meditation, the practice of holiness, charity, the avoidance of major vices, slander, selfishness and thankfulness to god for all His gifts. While pursuing good works one must avoid pride, arrogance and seek the grace of God with sincerity and devotion.

There are so many distractions and temptations in life; one must seek the company of spiritual and good people. Which will give him both courage and inspiration. It is impossible to understand god's mysteries. He controls the entire creation and it is good to surrender one's will to God's will. Those who contemplate God's power are lost in wonder. They seek to win His blessing by serving His creation and inspiring others to do the same. Sukhmani is a gem of spiritual aspiration and wisdom. Teja Singh, Lou Singh and others have translated it into English.

Anand Sahib

It is a poetical composition of Guru Amar Das included in the Guru Granth Sahib. It consists of 40 stanzas. The word "Anand" means permanent joy and bliss. Worldly prayer, wealth and position do not give joy or happiness; on the contrary, they produce fear, tension, pride and loss of peace of mind. The ideal goal of man is spiritual fulfilment or being in tune with the Almighty. The hurdles in the spiritual path are egoism, family attachment, desires, hypocrisy and social compulsions, but the can be controlled by following the Guru's instructions. Bliss is attained through self-discipline and the development of one's own personality through contentment, compassion, morality and social service.

The Anand assures every one that he can experience tranquillity and peace of mind without sacrificing the normal comforts and pleasures of life. Bliss is the ultimate destiny of man. Pain and suffering, though unavoidable, do not disturb the inner peace of that person who leads a pious life according to the Guru's instructions contained in the sacred hymns. The Anand is composed in Ramkali Rag, which leaves a powerful impression on the mind, and also explains clearly difficult concepts like Hukam, Nirmal, Punn, and Maya etc. It is recited at the end of every Sikh wedding service in its abbreviated form (first five and last stanzas). It is also recited at the end of every religious service before Ardas, and thereafter Hukam is taken and Karah Parsad (consecrated pudding) is distributed among the congregation.

Ardas

Ardas (petition) is a prayer recited at the conclusion of Sikh rituals. In modern times the Ardas prayer includes the invocation from Chandi ki var, which is mandatory, and is the only portion, which has not been changed. It is believed that the Singh Sabha composed most of the modern text of the Ardas in the beginning of the twentieth century, and that is why it contains a lot of verses connecting it with the Khalsa. The last verses contain religious discourse. The word Khalsa at the time of Guru Gobind Singh meant pure person. Bhai Santokh Singh in Sri Gur Pratap Suraj Granth, published by Khalsa Samchar in March, 1933, p.5608, in the footnote gives the following meaning of Khalsa: (Kha means yog or jap, L means bhog mahin, and Sa means sagar hane majh or mel). Thus Khalsa implied yog+bhog+mel or spirituality, worldly enjoyment and unity, all combined into one. These qualities are only available in saint soldier.

The following is the text of the Ardas prayer:

Victory to the One Almighty. May the God help. Ode to God by the tenth Guru. Remember first the Almighty and then Guru Nanak, Guru Angad, Guru Amar Das and Guru Ram Das. May the God and the Gurus protect us.

Turn your thoughts to Guru Arjan Dev, Guru Hargobind and Guru Har Rai. Meditate on Sri Guru Harkishan a sight of who dispels all sorrows and miseries.

Remember Guru Teg Bahadur and all the treasure of the world comes rushing to your home. May the saintly Gurus help us everywhere.

Turn your thoughts on the Divine light of the Tenth Guru and the Guru Granth Sahib, and get happiness from the sight of Guru Granth Sahib, and say glory to the God.

Khalsa Ji say glory to the God and think of the deeds of the Five beloved ones, the four sons of the tenth Guru, brave Sikhs who gave their lives for the faith, who remembered the Name and ate together in the free kitchen, who fought Dharm Yudh, who overlooked other's shortcomings. All these were true devotees.

Khalsa Ji say glory to the God and remember the great service rendered by those brave men as well as women who sacrificed their lives but did not surrender their faith. Remember them as well who got their limbs cut one by one, who were tied and rotated on the wheels, cut by saws, flayed alive, sacrificed their lives to keep their faith to their last breath.

Turn your thoughts to the five seats of Sikh religion (Takhats) and all the Sikhs temples, and say glory to the Almighty.

Khalsa Ji all of you turn your thoughts to meditate on God's Name and may all pleasures and meditation comes through such meditation.

Almighty give your protection to Khalsa. May the free

kitchen and sword never fail. Maintain the honour and victory to your devotees. May the respected sword always come to our help and Khalsa (pure people or purity) get respected. Say glory to the God.

Kindly bless the Sikhs the gift of learning their faith (keep long hair, obey laws, divine knowledge, faith, belief, meditate on the God's name, and bath in the tank of nectar at Amritsar)

O God! May the choirs, the mansion and the banner exist forever, and may the truth always win. Glory to the God.

O God you are the protector of wisdom. May the minds of all the Sikhs remain humble and their wisdom exalted.

O Immortal God, constant helper of the Sikhs, kindly confer the gift of visiting, maintaining, controlling and worshipping, without any restrictions, the Gurdwara of Nankana Sahib, other Gurdwaras, and Gurus mansions, of which the Khalsa has been deprived by the partition of India.

O Immortal God you are the honour of the meek, the power of the helpless, the shelter of the shelter less, we humbly pray to your to forgive our faults in reciting the Guru Grant Sahib.

Kindly fulfil our objects and bring peace and prosperity to all. Allow us to meet true devotees so that we may meditate upon Your Name. Through Guru Nanak may Your Name be exalted, and may all prosper according to Your Will.

Khalsa (pure) belongs to God and as such victory will be of God's.

Asa di Var

It literally means ballad of hope. It is a composition of Guru Nanak and Guru Angad under Rag Asa in Guru Granth Sahib. It is sung in a Sikh congregation as a morning prayer. The musicians sing this Var along with Chhands (quatrains) of Guru Ram Das. Asa di Var consists of 24 stanzas (pauris) and 44 staves (slokas). Its theme is: how to become a spiritual person. The disciple has to remove the obstacles that lie in the spiritual path, namely, ego, religiosity, bigotry, and exploitation. Humility and love are the most effective qualities for keeping people away from sin. God reads our heart and is not won by religious ceremonies, alms giving or penance or physical torment.

Guru Nanak rejected the idea of pollution connected with events of birth and death. These are natural events ordained by god. Real pollution is self-incurred; it comes from greed, lying, lust and slander, all of which corrupt the mind. Real impurity does not exist in food, but in one's ego, in neglect of our fellowmen and forgetfulness of god. In Asa di Var the Guru Nanak praises the role of women in family life. Why she should be called low or inferior? All human beings are equal and worthy of respect.

Guru Nanak's message in this Var is that there is no spiritual merit in activities like fasting, pilgrimage and penance. On the social side, caste pride, greed, hypocrisy are also rejected. The tyranny of rulers and the priestly class is challenged as a threat to peace and harmony in society. The Guru praised the wonders of nature and the pervasive spirit of god, His sovereignty and His grace. It is only by surrender and submission to god; one can win the favour of the creator. The singing of Asa di Var in the early morning or listening to it brings sense of peace and joy to a seeker of truth.

Diversity in Sikh Panth (sect or community or system of religious society or denominations)

The Sikhism is of two kinds: the simple theism of Guru Nanak which was marked by no outward signs, and saint-soldier faith of Guru Gobind Singh which was indicated by Pahul (baptism) and keeping five k's (1).Kesh—unshorn hair (2) Kangha, comb (3) Kara—steel wrist band (4) Kach, underpants (5) and Karpan—steel sword, and certain customs such as abstinence from tobacco, alcohol and the assumption of the title of a Singh. Some devotees also believed in the continuity of Guruship and started their own sect of the Sikhs. The following are examples of diversity within the Sikh Panth.

Akali

The Akali or Nihang owe their origin to the patronage of Guru Gobind Singh. The Akali means immortal, as he is the follower of the immortal god (Akal Purukh). The usual account of Akali origin is that Guru Gobind Singh seeing his infant son playing before him with his turban peaked in the fashion now adopted by the Akalis, blessed his son and instituted a sect which would follow the same custom.

The Akalis differ from all other orders in being a militant organisation. Some wear a yellow turban beneath the blue one, so as to show a yellow band across the forehead. The story goes that a Khatri of Delhi (and Lal, author of Zindaginama) desired to see the Guru in yellow, and Guru Gobind Singh fulfilled his wish. Many Sikhs wear yellow turban on Basant Panchami festival. Once Bhai Gurdas (first cousin of the mother of Guru Arjan, died 1629) said: (Suhi sufed jo pahne, Surkhh, zarde, soi bhai.) It means that all the Sikhs are Guru Bhai (followers of the Sikh Gurus), and it does not matter whether they wear dark blue clothes like the Akali Sikhs or white like the Nirmnals or red like the Udasis.

The term Akali is said to be derived from Akal Purush (worshipper of the eternal God), and Akali is simply a God's worshipper. The Akalis wear blue-chequered dresses, and bangles or bracelets of steel. Around their wrists, quoits of steel in their lofty conical blue turbans, together with miniature daggers, knives, and an iron chain. An Akali who wishes to imply that he is alone means that he is equivalent to 125,000 (sava lakh).

In their military capacity the Akalis were called Nihangs, and played a considerable part in the Sikh history in forming the Shahidi (martyrs) Misal. The Akali headquarters are the Akal Bunga at Amritsar, where they assumed the direction of religious ceremonies and the duty of involving the

Gurmata; they laid claim to exercise a general leadership of the Khalsa. The Sikh chiefs, from whom they often levied contributions by force, dreaded them. Maharaja Ranjit Singh of the Panjab, after 1823, did much to reduce their power, and the order lost its importance. The Akalis are celibate. They do not eat meat or partake of spirits, as other Sikhs do, but consume inordinate quantities of bhang (hemp).

Jagiasi

Sindhi Hindus are known by their two sects (Jagiasi and Udasi) from two sons of Guru Nanak (Sri Chand and Lakshmi Chand). The word Jagiasi is a Sindhi variant of a Sanskrit word jijnasu meaning desire to know or thought. This is a religious sect of Sindhi Hindus who are Nanakpanthi (followers of Guru Nanak). The Sindhi Hindus have followed the teachings of Guru more closely and claim to be more secular. Among Sindhi's there are some who add Singh to their names and have accepted the baptism of Guru Gobind Singh. Of the 23 Lakh Sindhis in India today, the Lohanas (meaning people made of iron) are numerous. They are originally from Kshatriya class, but they are also called Baniyas because of their interest in business and trade. Masands or tex collectors of the Guru were mostly recruited from this class. The famous temple of Sadhubelo in Sukur city (now Pakistan) belonged to Jagiasis. Baba Gurpat Rai was sent to Sindh by Maharaja Ranjit Singh and he built many Jagiasi temples there. He was known as a saint and he treated Hindus and Muslims alike. Jagiasi and Nanakpanthis are the same in the manner of beliefs and practices of worship. They employ Brahmins to perform their religious rites. They do readings from the Adi Granth and also from Vedas, Ramayana and Gita etc. In Jagiasi temple they listen to the Adi Granth in the morning and Ramaya and Gita in the evening. They believe in Lord Ram and Lord Krishna and also follow the teachings of Adi Granth. They also worship Hindu gods and wear sacred thread, and observe all Hindu rites and a Brahmin officiates at the ceremonies connected with their birth, marriage and death. Their women also observe Hindu fasts like Karwa Chauth etc.

Kukas or Namdharis or Naindharis

An Udasi Arora founded a Sikh sect called Kukas or "shouters", in the middle of the 19th century. His principal object has been to break the powers, which the Brahmans had acquired over the Sikh religion. After his death the doctrines of the sect were disseminated by a carpenter named Ram Singh, who proclaimed that he was an incarnation of Guru Gobind Singh (Tenth Guru). He prohibited all sort of worship except reading the Granth, and established his headquarters at Baini (Ludhiana District). The other headquarter of the sect is in Jiwan Nagar (Haryana). Ram Singh had a quarrel with the British and was deported to Rangoon (Burma), where he died in 1887. His brother Budh Singh succeeded him. The sect is known as Kukas or shouters as they fall into a state of frenzy during their religious prayers, by shaking their heads and reciting their prayers in a loud voice. They finish their prayers by speaking loudly Sat Sri Akal (God is the only truth). They also call themselves Namdharis. The true Khalsa should carry a staff in his hand, tie his turban in a fashion called Sidha Pag (straight turban), and wear a woollen necklace tied in knots. These signs have almost fallen in disuse. They are forbidden to eat meat or drink spirits or smoke tobacco.

They were the sworn enemies of the British rule in India, but on the other hand, Akalis had been great favourites of the British for recruitment into the army. They believe in the Guru Granth Sahib and also the Daswan Granth of the Guru Gobind Singh, but also have faith in the living Guru. They do not accept the Guru Granth Sahib as their Guru. They worship their living Guru. They do not take Khand-di-pahul or baptism of Guru Gobind Singh. They prepare their own food and do not accept it from others. The living Guru always initiates a new disciple by giving him a mantra.

Kukas believe in an inexpensive marriage ceremony and are forbidden by their faith to have marriage ceremonies conducted at home. Every Kuka is supposed to marry his son or daughter at a religious fair in the presence of Satguru. Many marriages take place at one such fair. A Havan is performed before the marriage ceremony.

The couple takes bath early in the morning and is brought to the congregation where the Asa Di Var is being sung. Both the bride and groom get dressed in white. The bride puts a woollen rosary around the neck of the bridegroom, as a mark of respect and touches his feet. They get baptised with the Amrit (nectar, water of immortality) already prepared and the marriage ceremony begins. The couple gets around the sacred fire four times while the priest reads verses from the Holy Granth. They are not allowed to hold post-marriage parties or any other ceremony at home. Vegetarian food is offered to everyone who attends the marriage and charges for Havan are nominal for the ingredients (samagri) used for lighting the holy fire. The sect believes in the world peace.

Minas

It means cunning, wicked, etc. A nickname given by the Sikh Gurus to those who pretended to become Gurus, while they were unfit to become Gurus. The word Mina was first used by Bhai Gurdas (first cousin of mother of Guru Arjan and Prithi Chand) for Prithi Chand.

The second sect of the Sikhs was Minas. Ram Das (4th Guru) had three sons (Prithi Chand, Mahadev and Arjan). When the eldest son (Prithi Chand) of the Guru did not get Guruship, he started a sect called Minas. He had followers whom he warned against association with the Sikhs of Guru Arjan Dev. Enmity between both sects has existed up to the present day. Miharban, the son of Prithi Chand, wrote a biography of Guru Nanak in which he glorified his own father. Bhai Gurdas has described the characteristics of Mina in Var 36. They are like counterfeit coins, similar in appearance, but made of different stuff or substance. Their minds are corrupt and evil. In the Rahitnama and Rahat Maryada, there is ban on Sikhs for any relationship or association with Minas (descendants of Prithi Chand).

Misal/Misl system of Sikhs

In Sikhism Misal means "the various clans under their respective chiefs, leagued together to form a confederacy" implying that chiefs and followers of one clan were equal to those of another. It also means a clan or a voluntary association of autonomous Sikh chiefs united in a league for a common purpose. Between 1748 and 1761 the Panjab was invaded three times by Ahmad Shah Abdali. In 1758 Marhattas and the Sikhs drove Ahmad Shah Abdali out of Lahore, but in 1761 they were completely defeated by Ahmad Shah Abdali, who later retired to Kabul. Gradually the power of the Sikhs increased and they grouped themselves into associations, called Misals, on democratic and equal basis. This organisation made them powerful. Many chiefs of the Misals built their forts in convenient places, and gradually overran the whole plain country of the Panjab.

The initiated Sikhs, who had taken Pahul (baptism), formed the Khalsa (the chosen, elect or pure), the commonwealth of states of the Guru. The Sarbat Khalsa (all the Sikh people) met once at least at Amritsar during Diwali. The commonwealth was organised into a number of Misals (confederacies). These Misals were loosely organised and varied from time to time in power, and even in designation. There were usually known as eight Misals and four Dehras or camps. The following were the Sikh Misals, and class from which they were mainly recruited.

1. Bhangis. They were all Jats from Amritsar, Taran Taran, Gujrat, Wazirabad, Sialkot and Chiniot. Chajja Singh, a companion of Banda Bahadur, led the Misal. It was the strongest Misal, but ultimately Ranjit Singh annexed

the territory of Bhangi Misal.

2. Nishania or Nishanwala, or standard bearer from Nishan (standard). They were mostly Khatris and Rangretta from Ambala. The founder of this Misal was Dasaunda Singh and Sangat Singh. After 1800 Ranjit Singh amalgamated this Misal with his own territory.
3. Ramgarhia, from Ramgarh, a village near Amritsar. They were mostly Tarkhans (carpenters) and Jats. They were mainly from Hargobindpur, Batala and Mukerian. The founder of the Misal was Jassa Singh Ramgarhia. He was succeeded by his son (Jodh Singh) who submitted to Ranjit Singh.
4. Ahluwalia. From Ahlu, a village near Lahore. They were mainly from Kapurthala, Nurmahal,Talwandi, Phagwara and Haryana. Jassa Singh Ahluwalia was the founder of the Misal, and Fateh Singh was the last leader of the Misal
5. Kanhaiya or Ghania, from Ghani, a village near Lahore. They were mainly from Gurdaspur, Ajnala, Sohiyan, Dehra Baba Nanak and Pathankot. Jai Singh founded this Misal, and he got his granddaughter (Mehtab Kaur) married to Ranjit Singh. After some time Ranjit Singh amalgamated this Misal with his own Sukra Chakia Misal.
6. Faizalpuria or Singhpuriya. They were mainly Jats from Jalandhar, Habitpur and Patri. Kapur Singh of Faizalpur village founded it. He was succeeded by Budh Singh and after his death Ranjit Singh took over his territory.
7. Sukra Chakia Misal. Mainly Jats from Gujranwala, Kunja etc.
8. Dalewalia. They were mainly Jats from Nakodar, Talban, Rahon and Philour, etc. Gulab Singh of village Dalewalia (near Sultanpur) was the founder of this Misal. He took part in expeditions against Ahmad Shah Abdali. His successor was Tara Singh, and on his death, Ranjit Singh took over the territory.

Four Dehras (camps) of Misals

1. Shahids (martyrs). Mainly Jats from Shahzadpur. .
2. Nakkias, from Nakka. Mainly Jats from Chunian, Bahrwal, Khemkaran and Khudian.
3. Panjgarhias or Krora Singhias, who were divided into (a) Sham Singhan and (b) Kalsias, the later is further subdivided into Laudpindian and Bara Pindian or Birk and Jabalian. Their capital was Bunga, and they were mainly from Nawanshahr, Rurka, Bassian, Pindorian, Hoshiarpur, Banga and Kathgarh.
4. Phulkian. They were Jats mainly from Nabha and Patiala.

The rise of Ranjit Singh and his policy of taking over the land of Misals made the Sikh empire possible on the ruins of Misaldhari system in Panjab.

Namdeo Panthi

Baba Namdeo a disciple of Ramanand, was born in Marwar AD 1443. Muslims, who tried to persuade him to repeat the words "Allah-Allah", instead of his favourite "Ram, Ram", persecuted him but by a variety of astonishing miracles he escaped from their hands. He came to Panjab and settled in the village of Ghumman (Gurdaspur district), where he died. A shrine known as the Darbar, was erected in honour of Baba Namdeo in Ghuman, and on the Sankarant fast day of every Magh (January-February), a big fair is held in his honour. He taught the unity of God and the uselessness of ceremonies; and his doctrine are close to that of Guru Nanak. Several of his poems are included in the Guru Granth Sahib. The followers of Baba Namdeo are mostly Sikhs. The Hindu Namdeo Panthis also hold the Guru Granth Sahib in reverence.

Namdhari sect (of Naushehra Majha Singh)

The leader of the sect in the year 2000 was Sant Harnam Singh of Naushehra Majha Singh. It is a part of the original Kuka or Namdhari movement. The other group at present is led by Guru Jagjit Singh. Both groups believed in Baba Ram Singh as their original Guru who started the movement.

Sant Harnam Singh was born in a Khatri family in 1877 at Qilla Sooba Singh in Sialkot district (Pakistan). As a young man he joined the Namdhari sect and went to Bhaini Sahib for meditation. After getting enlightenment at Bhaini Sahib, he returned to his village. Most of the Khatri community of his village became his followers. He delivered them Gurumantra and made them Namdhari. The villagers treated him as their Guru and ignored the main Namdhari Guru at Bhaini Sahib. After the partition of India in 1947, Sant Harnam Singh came to Naushehra Majha Singh, a village near Batala.

The distinctive feature of the new Namdhari is their uniform. The original uniform is a white kurta (shirt), white pyjama (trouser), and a white turban tied in a special way. They also carry lathi (sticks). The new Namdhari sect of Sant Harnam Singh has substituted a blue piece of cloth tied in a particular style for the white turban and has added a blue waistband to the uniform. The use of lathi (stick) has been discontinued. Sela (a kind of hook) is used to dig the ground (before one eases oneself) in villages where home toilets are not available. They also use Mala (a chain of small diamond shaped stones) for the purpose of meditation.

The followers of the sect are not allowed to eat meat, wine or drugs. They also are not supposed to eat food cooked by non-followers.

At Naushehra Majha Singh there are two Gurdwaras in the village. The one outsid the village is used for festivals and the other in the village is used for daily prayers.

They have some branches in India, Singapore and Bangkok. The sect believes in the Guru Granth Sahib and their living Guru. Occasionally when the Guru sits with his Followers, they clap their hands and dance around him. The sect believes in social work and financial help to the poor. They celebrate Hola. Amawas (night of the complete darkness), the birthday of Baba Ram Singh (founder of the sect), Sankrant (first day of each month), Puranmashi (night of the full moon), and birthday of the Sikh Gurus.

Nanak Panthi

They are the followers of Guru Nanak. They were taught about the unity of God, the uselessness of ceremonies, the vanity of earthly wishes and the equality of castes, topics that are common to Guru Nanak and the contemporary's saints (Bhagats). The Guru Granth Sahib is full of quotations from elder or contemporary saints/teachers, who taught doctrine as Nanak himself.

The Nanak Panthis of the sixteenth and seventeenth centuries were a sect much as the Kabir Panthis and the Dadu Panthis are sects. The Nanak Panthis of today are known as Sikhs who are not Singhs, who do not think it necessary to follow the ceremonies and social observances inculcated by Guru Gobind Singh. They do not forbid smoking, or keep long hairs, or the five Ks (Panj Kakkas), they are not baptised with the Khande di pahul, they do, not look on the Brahmans as superfluity, and so forth. They are also known as Sahijdhari—followers of Guru Nanak. The term Nanak Panthi is applied in a very loose way. The followers of Nanak also call themselves as Nanak Shahi, Nanak Dasi, Sewak Guru Nanak, Nanak Math, and Baba Panthi etc.

Nihang

It means free from care. It is a title of Akali Sikhs. (See also Akali). It also means a person without pride or arrogance, a humble and gentle person. Nihang Singhs trace their origin to the creation of the Khalsa by Guru Gobind Singh and consider themselves to be his true Khalsa (soldiers of the Eternal One, or Akal Purukh). The Nihangs are divided into four groups or Dals (Tarna Dal, Baba Bidi Chand Dal, Baba Bhindran Dal and Baba Budha Dal). Within each Dal all members are equal except for the Jathedar who is the supreme commander of the Dal and he will nominate his successor.

The philosophy of the Nihang is that of Raja Yogi (holy man) and yet involved in the affairs of the world. Some Nihangs get married and some stay unmarried. Most of them stay at Nihang Dera (settlement next to a Gurdwara). They till the land given to them. The income from the land is used for langar (free kitchen). Nihangs take part in all Sikh festivals in order to serve the people. They wear blue clothes. They believe that God likes the blue colour and that is why the sky, the purified flames of a fire and the water—all are blue. A Nihang wears a blue turban called a damala. There is a farla on top of the turban, which is like a big flag. They wear iron rings around their turbans. These rings are called chakkars, are like stars on an officer's shoulders. As a Nihang makes progress in the spiritual life, the chakkars are placed higher and higher on their turbans. If the chakkar is on the top of the turban it symbolises his having achieved a very high degree of enlightenment. They wear a long blue shirt which they call a chola. They also keep a comb in their hair and wear a long underwear (shorts). They also keep a sword with them. Nihangs do not drink, but they take bhang (hemp), which they call Sukh Nidhan (treasure of bliss). They believe that bhang (hemp) helps them to meditate and concentrate. They believe that liquor is of no use in meditation as it makes one depressed; however they do not object to the use of liquor by others. (J.C.B Webster. Popular religions in the Punjab today. P. 40-45. Batala, The Christian of Sikh Studies, 1974.)

Niranjani

The sect was founded in the sixteenth century by Baba Handal, who was cook and tax collector to Guru Amar Das (3rd Guru), and worshipped the Almighty under the name of Niranjan (The Bright One). His followers are known as Niranjanis. They are rapidly declining in numbers. Those who still exist are found chiefly in the Jalandhar, Amritsar and Kapurthala districts.

Their chief claim to notice is their rejection of the ordinary funeral ceremonies of the Sikhs and the Hindus. They reject all funeral rites (kiria karam), and do not send the ashes of their dead to the Ganges. They have special marriage rites of their own and do not reverence Brahmans. Their principal shrine is at Jandiala.

Nirmals

Nirmal Sadhus (pure saints) are a Sikh order which was bitterly opposed to the Akalis. They do not go under any rites of purification, but receive Amrit like other Sikhs when they become Singhs, but the history of their foundation is obscure. According to one story, the Guru's soldiers seized a water carrier for supplying water to the enemy soldiers during a battle, but the Guru appreciated his work and declared him stainless (Nirmal). Guru Gobind Singh sent many of his followers to learn Sanskrit. They wore the saffron clothes of the sadhus (saints) and translated many Sanskrit works into Panjabi. These people were known as Nirmals by the Guru. Another story is that once after a hard fought battle, Guru Gobind Singh and his companion were sleeping, but at midnight the Guru woke up to see if any were awake in meditation. Those whom he found keeping vigil in spite of their fatigue, he called them Nirmals.

At first the Nirmals accepted pahul and wore white raiment, but they have adhered to the study of the orthodox Hindu scriptures and therefore lost touch with Sikhism. They now wear ordinary saffron robes of the Indian faqir. All Nirmals are Keshdghari (keep long hairs). The Nirmals are a well-disciplined and highly respected organisation. Each monastery is under a Guru, while a council or committee periodically visits their societies through the province. Almost all of them are celibate; they bear a far higher respect for morality than most of the other religious orders in the Panjab. Their principal Akhara (headquarter) is at Haridwar, but they have foundations at Amritsar and elsewhere in the Panjab.

The precise derivation of the name Nirmal is obscure. The Yogis practise a rite called nivali or niuli (physical purification by purging) as a preliminary to the rite of Yoga (drawing in breath), and the term Nirmal may be derived from this practice.

Nirankari Sikhs

The follower of the Nirankari movement believe that Bhai Dayal Das, founder of the movement, brought the Sikhs to their original loyalty taught by the Gurus. The Nirankari Sikhs are liberal and profess the true mission of Guru Nanak. They believe in the Guru Granth Sahib, and also in existence of a living teacher and guide.

It is a Sikh sect founded by Bhai Dayal Das, a Khatri of Peshawar, who established Rawalpindi about 1845. On his death in 1870 his son, Bhai Darbara Singh succeeded him, and then Bhai Ratta, another son. Later Bhai Ratta's son, Sahib Gurdit Singh, continued the propogation of the Nirankari mission until 1947.

After the partition of India, Nirankari's migrated to India leaving behind their main centre in Rawalpindi and more than sixty sub-centres in Pakistan. A new centre has been established at Chandigarh. The fifth Satguru of the Nirankaris, Sahib Hara Singh (1877-1971) started reorganising the sangat. His eldest son Baba Gurbakhsh Singh succeeded him.

The Nirankaris worship one invisible God as a spirit who is a hearer of prayer, avoiding idols, and making no offerings to them, the Brahmans or to the dead. They abstain from partaking of flesh and liquor and reverence truth. Pilgrimages are regarded as useless, and neither Brahmans nor cows are to be revered. The first day of each week is to be kept holy by attendance at the temple, reading the

Granth, repentance for sins, and almsgiving. The Adi Granth of Baba Nanak is their sacred book, though they also respect the later Gurus and their writings. The weddings are celebrated according to Sikh rites, by a Sikh priest (Granthi). The bride sits unveiled in public and the bride and groom circumambulate the Adi Granth. They believe in transmigration of soul, reverence towards parents and elders. At funerals they do not mourn. Smoking is forbidden, but may sell or deal in tobacco. The use of wine and flesh is forbidden. Besides the usual Sikh places of pilgrimages the Nirankaris look with special reverence upon a pool in the park at Rawalpindi (Pakistan) to which they have given the name Amritsar.

A breakaway sect emerged in the 1930s under the leadership of one Buta Singh and soon became more popular than the parent Nirankari body. Though denounced as nakli (artificial), Buta Singh's son, Avtar Singh, acquired a very large following and compiled two scriptures for the sect: Avtar Bani and Yug Purush. Orthodox Sikhs strongly resented certain passages in these texts, which they felt denigrated the Sikh Gurus and the Guru Granth Sahib. Nirankaris believe in a living Guru. The Akal Takht excommunicated the sect in 1970.

Ramgarhias or Tarkhans (carpenter)

Sikh Tarkhan always call themselves Ramgarhias in remembrance of a famous ancestor called Jassa Singh, who was the leader of the Ramgarhia missal (confederacy), and the builder of Ramgarh, a fortress near Amritsar. Tradionally a Tarkhan (Ramgarhia) manufacture and repairs agricultural implements and household furniture required in his village. At present many Ramgarhias are cultivators and hold respectable positions in all walks of life (engineering, medicine and technology etc). The main sects of the clan are: Dhamma, Khatti, Siawan, Matharu, Gade, Tharu Natal, Janjua and Khokar. At present Ramgarhia community has separate Gurdwaras and do not like to marry their children with Sikh Jat communities.

Ravidasi, Ramdasi, Raodasi or Raidasi

They are the followers of Guru Nanak and other Gurus. In its widest sense Ramdasi means a follower of Guru Ram Das and other Gurus. The followers are Chamars (dealer of hides and leather) and weavers. Saint Ravi Das (Chamar) was a disciple of Ramanand and was born at Banaras and his followers are mainly low caste (Chamars). Ravidasi followers do not take pahul (baptism) and most of them believe only in Guru Nanak and his writings.

They are taught about the unity of God, forbade the worship of idols; believe in the uselessness of ceremonies, the vanity of earthly wishes and the equality of castes, topics that are common to Guru Nanak and the contemporary's saints (Bhagats). The Guru Granth Sahib is full of quotations from elder or contemporary saints/teachers, who taught doctrine as Nanak himself. Ravidasi have their separate temples

Udasi

The first sect of the Sikhs began immediately after the demise of Guru Nanak. Some of his followers adopted Sri Chand, the elder son of Guru Nanak, as his successor, and rejected Guru Angad as the second Guru. The followers of Sri Chand were and known as Udasis (the solitary) and they now are a large number of pious and earnest men. Anand, an Udasi, has written a biography of Guru Nanak. It states that Sri Chand was an incarnation of God, and the only true successor of Guru Nanak.

The Udasi sect is an ascetic order, they pay special reverence to the Adi Granth. Their service consists of ringing the bells and the blare of instruments, the chanting of hymns and the waving of lights before the Adi Granth and the portrait of Guru Nanak. They Are not uniform in their customs. Some wear long hairs, some short, and some wear caste marks. The head of each Udasi brotherhood is called a Mahant and his disciples are called chelas (disciples). The dress of the sect is of red colour, but many go naked except for a waist cloth., and rub ashes all over their bodies. Their principal shrine is at Dera Baba Nanak in Gurdaspur District.

Army, Sikh

Due to personal jealousies of Sikhs chieftains they could not become a formidable army in Northern India as the Mahratas could in the south and west India. The democratic nature of the Sikh faith resisted all attempts at dictation by a central authority, until Maharaja Ranjit Singh broke down all opposition, and reduced rivals and enemies to a common obedience. The history of the Sikhs from the middle of the 18th to the beginning of the 19th century is a record of struggles, for pre-eminence among the chiefs of the different Misals (Sikh clans or groups) who fought against each other than their common enemy Muslim. In 1797 Lahore was held by three Sikhs chiefs and in 1798 Zaman Shah brought an army from Kabul and got Lahore without any opposition. Due to troubles at home he gave the control of the city to a young Ranjit Singh who had rendered him valuable service. Ranjit Singh was illiterate but a man of strong will, great intelligence and determination. He united all Misls or Sikh chieftains under his own control and became the chief of the Sikhs of Panjab. From 1808 to 1813 he became the Maharaja of Panjab, Himachal Pradesh and Kashmir. In the same year he obtained from Shah Shuja, the fugitive Amir of Kabul, what he coveted as much as territory –the celebrated Koh-I-Nur diamond, which Nadir Shah had carried off as loot from Delhi.

The Sikh army was generally known as the Dal Khalsa (Army of Pure or God). It consisted for the most part of cavalry, who found their own horses, and received a double share of prize money. Each chief, in proportion to his means furnished horses and arms to his retainers, who were called Bargirs; and as the first tribute exacted from a conquered district was invariably horses, the infantry soldier was, after a successful campaign, generally transformed into a trooper. The infantry, previous to the formation of a regular, by Ranjit Singh, was considered an inferior service. The only people who were considered worthy were Akalis (immortals or saint soldiers) who dressed in blue, and wore knife-edged quoits round their turbans, partly for show during peace time, and party to use as a missile during war.

Ranjit Singh had formed several battalions, drilled chiefly by men who had resigned or deserted from the East India Company's service. His troops consisted Hindustanis (Hindus, Muslims and Sikhs) and Gorkhas of Nepal. The artillery was chiefly composed of Muslims. The Akali Sikhs did not like the rigidity and precision of the infantry drill, and it is only by liberal pay Ranjit Singh made them to submit to the European system of discipline.

During the Maharaja's reign, enlistment in the regular army was voluntary, being composed to strongest young men. Under the Maharaja the Khalsa battalions became a formidable body of troops. Their endurance was remarkable and it was not unusual for whole regiments to make 30 miles marches for many days continuously.

Following the examples of Maharaja of Scindia and Holkar, Ranjit Singh employed French and Italian officers to improve artillery. French and Italian were not allowed to command them in the field, as these were reserved for his own Indian Generals. Of all the Generals of Maharaja, Diwan Mokhan Chand, Diwan Chand, Hari Singh Nalwa, Gulab Singh were the ablest and had a distinguished career.

Ranjit Singh died in 1839, was succeeded by Kharak Singh, his eldest son, a weak and incapable prince, under whose rule the history of the Panjab became a record of intrigues and deeds of violence. The regime of Kharak Singh and his son Nao Nihal Singh were short lived. Kharak Singh was assassinated and his son died by the fall of a beam from the gateway. They were succeeded by two other sons of Ranjit Singh (1) Sher Singh was murdered, and (2) Dalip Singh, an infant, was brought to the U.K.

Ranjit Singh left an army of 92,000 infantry, 32,000 cavalry, and nearly 400 guns. It was a force, which his week successors could not control. When all the successors were killed and the treasury plundered, the army unpaid and unmanageable. Under these circumstances Panjab was annexed by the British.

In 1846 orders were issued by the British government for the formation of two Sikh battalions at Ferozpur and Ludhiana, and ten years later another regiment was raised. In 1849 the policy of, the British government, giving military employment to the Sikhs was yet extended by forming the corps of Guides and a brigade of all arms, for police and general purposes on the border, both of which were largely composed of the former soldiers of the Khalsa, and formed the nucleus of the Panjab Frontier Force.

During the mutiny of 1857 the Sikhs were told that Hindustani sepoys were trying to restore the Muslim rule. The Sikhs identified themselves with the British and took a prominent share in the suppression of the Mutiny.

Bhakti movement

During the medieval times Bhakti movement spread all over India. The idea of Bhakti movement was to reform Hinduism. The movement was based on truth and service to human beings. The movement offered people in (1) improving their social and spiritual life by joining it, (2) reducing bitterness between the followers of Hinduism and Islam, (3) interpreting Hinduism in such a way to make it more attractive than Islam to the lower classes which were getting converted in large numbers, (4) making untouchables more important members of Hindu society, and (5) making Hinduism very liberal and defend it and Hindus from attack by Islam.

Baba Namdeo, a disciple of Ramanand, was born in Marwar AD 1443. He was persecuted by Muslims, but escaped from their hands and settled in village Ghuman in district

Gurdaspur. He taught the unity of God and his doctrines are very close to Guru Nanak.

Namdev Bhagat (1270-1350) was born in Maharashtra brought Bhakti movement during the closing years of thirteenth century. His successors established branches in a number of places in Panjab and Jammu. They preached devotion to God as absolute and personal. It is believed that Guru Nanak might have got in touch with them during his journeys. The Hinduism preached that one can obtain salvation through (1) Giyan Marg (knowledge of holy scriptures), Karam Marg (good deeds), and Bhakti Marg (devotion). It was difficult for illiterate masses to practice the first two, but Bhakti Marg offered many practical things (devotion, contemplation, praise and prayer), and the method of salvation was open to all.

The Muslim rulers persecuted Hindus on account of idolatry and caste system, the saints of the Bhakti movement preached against both of them. Bhakti movement declared that there was only one God and all human beings were His children. Thus they preached the fatherhood of God and brotherhood of mankind. They said that God is one and you may call it Allah, Khuda, by Muslims and Ram or Parmatma by Hindus. In the eyes of God there was no person high or low, superior or inferior, big or small, rich or poor. They taught that all religions teach love of humanity, and for peace of mind—one should surrender to the Lord. They preached people at fairs, festivals, under shady trees and on occasions of marriages and mournings.

Before Nanak, Shakraacharya, Ramanuja, Namdev, Jaidev and Ramanand started Bhakti movements, and during Nanak's time the movement was spread by Kabir, Vallabacharya, Mira Bai, Chaitanya, and Tulsidas. Guru Nanak was also a great reformer who started Bhakti movement in Panjab. All these reformers attracted the Hindu people to get rid of bad beliefs, caste system and told them that good life and salvation will come by following the movement.

Sufi saints were very shrewd in following the principles of Bhakti movement. They sang and danced and adopted their teachings similar to the Bhakti movement and became very successful in converting millions of Hindus to Islam without force. They preached similar doctrines of peace and tolerance, and through their message of brotherly love and friendly co-operation, it became easier for them to convert illiterate, poor and depressed Hindus (lower classes) to Islam. The lower classes of Hindus did not know that by following the Sufis they were becoming Muslims. They believed that Sufis were the same as Hindus.

Guru Nanak, his teachings

The teachings of Guru Nanak are very important as a testimony to the continuity to the traditional teachings of the Guru and his successors. Guru Nanak could not describe God or feel Him, but He is everywhere. God is unborn, omnipresent, he creates the entire universe, and all things exist in Him. This divine essence is immaterial, invisible, unborn, uncreated, without beginning and without end, illimitable and inappreciable by the sense until the film of mortal blindness is removed. God creates the universe; it is dependent on Him and is in existence by His will. Nanak believed that God has created virtue and vice. A man should pursue the path of virtue.

Law of Karma (action, deed, duty, or acts obligatory on an individual) will prevail. Good actions will bore good fruit and bad action will bore bad fruit. Virtue provides happiness and vice brings misery. In Japji Nanak says: words do not make saint or sinner, and action alone is written in the book of fate. What we sow that alone we reap. Nanak believed in the transmigration of soul (Nirvan).

Like Hinduism Guru Nanak believed that soul never die. On the death of the body soul gets into a new body. There are eighty-four lakhs (840,0000) souls in existence and the number of human souls is only a fraction of creation. It marks a stage in the journey of the soul. The soul is a part of the God and it can never be destroyed. The soul is a divine spark and when it joins a body it becomes impure. To stay as a divine spark (ever lasting bliss, eternal happiness), one should always meditate on God, be virtuous and be helpful to all beings.

Nanak believed that Kam (lust), Karodh (anger), Lobh (greed), Moh (attachment), and Ahankar (conceit) are the five diseases from which all living beings were suffering. God has made human beings powerful enough to overcome them—any one who overcomes them is happiest of all.

God and his devotees are one and there is nothing between them. Guru Nanak summed up God in his Mul Mantra (basic formula).

Ik Omkar, Satnam Karta Purakh, Nirbhau Nirvair, Akalmurti, Ajuni, Saibhang, Gurprasad.

There is only one God, God is truth, He is the Creator, God is without fear, He is without animosity, and He is the immortal being. He is unborn. He is self-existent, God is realised by the grace of the Guru.
God belongs to all living beings, He can be realised through love, devotion and good deeds, He can be worshipped and realised by singing His praises and constant repetition of His Name. Guru Nanak taught Bhakti marg to reach God. In Hinduism and Sikhism it (Bhakti) signifies a union of implicit faith with incessant devotion to God. The doctrine of Bhakti was an important innovation upon the old Vedic religion. Bhakti, according to Guru Nanak is Nam-simaran (remembering the Holy Name or singing the praises of God). Guru Nanak believed that a true Guru (enlightener) could only lead a disciple to God.

Everybody else is subject to error; only the Guru and God are without error. In Sikhism Guru stands for God, for example, God was the Guru of Nanak. The Guru in Sikhism is both human and divine. In Adi Granth it is mentioned that "all utter Ram Ram, but one cannot get Ram by saying.

Ram (God) can live in heart with Guru's grace, only through Guru one can reach Ram (God). Guru Nanak demanded complete surrender from his disciple who would attain salvation through the superior spiritual power of the Guru.

In Japji Guru Nanak lays down the following five stages of spiritual progress:-

(a) Dharam khand—in this a disciple tries to discipline his mind and tries to establish contact with God.

(b) Gian khand—a disciple tries to gain knowledge and tries to understand the meaning of his existence in this world.

(c) Sharam khand—a disciple tries to reach God by meditation on his name.

(d) Karam khand—a disciple's virtuous life and his desire to reach God is appreciated by the Almighty.

(e) Sach khand— in which a disciple merges with God by meditating on His name.

Nanak says that in the soil of your mind sow the seed of good deeds and water the soil with God's name. The Guru believed that Grhastha Ashram (life of a householder) is the best way to reach God, and spiritual instruction essential to God and his devotees are one and there is nothing between them. Guru Nanak summed up God in his Mul Mantra (basic formula).

Ik Omkar, Satnam Karta Purakh, Nirbhau Nirvair, Akalmurti, Ajuni, Saibhang, Gurprasad.

Retain peace of mind. A teacher may be termed educated when he dispenses knowledge spontaneously, and always meditate on the name of God.

The Guru believed in charity and told his disciple that work is worship, practice Sahaj Yoga for mental peace and happiness, and love all beings and human beings irrespective of religion. He taught his disciples to stay clean, love god, resist evil, injustice, wickedness, earn by working, share earnings with the poor, and consider ill-gotten wealth as eating a corpse.

In Hinduism women are considered Goddess Lakshmi, an emblem of good luck and prosperity. The doctrine of Hindu religion has been singularly careful to protect the female sex and infants from violence, and it was unlawful to put a woman to death for any offence whatever. A Sanskrit sloka runs:

"Shut gao vudhe vepra,
Shut vepra vudhe istri,
Shut istria vudhea bala,.
Shut bala widhe muresha.

To kill one Brahman is equal to one hundred cows; to kill one woman is equal to one hundred Brahmans; to kill one child is equal to one hundred women; to kill; one hundred children is an offence too heinous for comparison.

In spite of the above sayings the women were held in inferior position, misused, kept in purdah/ Harim (female apartment of a Muslim household—where many wives stay together), and also child marriage and Sati were common. He tried to protect female sex from violence, gave them equal rights and was allowed to attend his sermons along with men as mentioned in Hindu scriptures. He condemned child marriage and Sati (self-immolation of widow on funeral pyre of husband). The Guru propagated that woman should be given a very high status as woman continues the race, tradition and give birth to king, queen, and there is no human being who is not born of women. He could not accept polygamous form of marriage of Muslims.

Guru Nanak believed in one God (Ik Omkar), faith in Guru and to lead a good householder's life. He did not denounce any religion; but he said that those who do not follow their religious scriptures are false. He denounced the caste system, but Ramanuja, Ramanand and Kabir had already rejected the caste system before him. The Guru rejected rituals and pilgrimages, but his followers did not reject completely. Mohsin Fani in his book (Dabistan p.223) says that Guru Nanak wore sacred thread of Hindus and did not reject it. He further says that a devoted disciple of Guru Har Govind, called Sadhu Ram, was wearing a sacred thread when he accompanied him from Kabul to Panjab after purchasing horses from Iran for the Guru. Like Hinduism, Guru Nanak believed in the law of Karma and transmigration of soul. He did not mind people eating meat, but he did not eat meat, and considered meat and wine unlawful. He established the institution of Sangat (congregation) like his predecessor Shankaracharya of eighth century.

Guru Nanak did not wish to hate the existing institutions of Hindus, Buddhist and Muslims, and he wanted to live in peace with them. He was a great reformer of Hinduism like Ramanuja, Ramanand and Kabir. He wanted to continue the Guruship started by him. Twenty days before his death on 2 September 1539 he decided to pass on the Guruship to his disciple Lahna and praised him in a big congregation. He placed five paise (pennies) and a coconut before Lahna, and gave him a collection of his own hymns and a rosary. He named him Angad (a part of his own body), appointed him his own successor, and declared that new Guru shared his spirit and soul as well. As a result the succeeding Gurus used the name Nanak in their compositions. Guru Nanak died on 22 September 1539, at Kartarpur and was known as Hindu ka Guru and Musalman ka Pir (Guru of Hindus and saint/Guru of Muslims).

Caste system

The Hindu society was based on castes. The Guru preached that the caste system was not based on divine love. They aimed at creating a casteless and classless society. The Guru's preached that a man's love of God should be the criterion to judge whether he was good or bad, high or low and not the caste. The highest and purest of all is the one whose mind dwells in the Lord. Guru Arjan gave four gates to Hari Mandar at Amritsar indicating that the Hari Mandar was open to all the four castes.

Economic and political life

Guru Arjan encouraged his followers to become traders in horses in addition to agriculture. This made them adventurous. In Dabistan-e Mazhib it is mentioned that some of the Sikh Guru take to agriculture and others to trade. The Muslim rulers treated the Hindus badly. The Gurus provided leadership to the Hindus and helped them to offer physical resistance to tyranny. Guru Hargobind and Guru Tegh Bahadur fought with the Muslim rulers. Aurangzeb had resolved to establish a purely Islamic state in India and to eliminate Hindus, and the last Guru Gobind Singh created Khalsa (pure and honest people as saint solders of unpaid army) to fight the emperor Aurangzeb.

The Sikh Gurus created national unity. They rejected caste system and encouraged women to work side by side with men. The Gurus taught that the human progress was based on the development of body, mind, social consciousness and spirituality. Spiritual freedom was not possible without political liberty. Many Jats and lower classes people became the followers of the Gurus as they gave them equality and dignity of a human being.

Manual labour, service and charity

Nanak worked as a cultivator at Kartarpur, Angad carried heavy loads of grass on his head. Amar Das brought a pitcher of water from river Beas, 5 kms distance, for Guru Angad's bath. Ram Das carried basket of earth on his head during the digging of well at Goindwal. Many Sikhs including Guru provided free labour for digging tanks. Thus the Gurus raised the dignity of manual labour. The Gurus placed before their Sikhs the ideal of service and sacrifice. Guru Nanak in Sri Rag says t hat the service of mankind is a warrant to heaven. Charity became essential for the Sikhs, as the money was required to run free kitchen and buy swords and horses to fight the Muslims. It became essential that every Sikh must contribute one-tenth of his earnings in the service of the community. It still exists to a certain extent on voluntary basis. The Guru also raised the status of women. The third Guru appointed a woman in charge of Manjhi (head of a congregation). They enjoyed equal rights with men.

Repetition of God's name

The Guru's taught that the God is everywhere and is present in everything. He listens to people's grievances and helps them. Salvation can only be obtained by repeating God's name. Bhakti tradition of the Hindus insisted on congregation system, which was adopted by the Guru's. Sangat or congregation has been an essential part of Sikh tradition. Langar (free kitchen) or eating together by all the castes in the Gurdwara was strictly enforced by the Gurus. This led to the amalgamation of all the castes into one class. Guru Amar Das invited all his followers on Baisakhi and Diwali day

(March-April and October-November). The later Gurus continued the practice. It enabled them to develop a spirit of fellow feelings.

Barah Maha of Guru Nanak

This work of Guru Nanak teaches how to be in love with the Lord. There is only one way to worship God. It is to extol him, to glorify him, to sing his praise, to take, believe and repeat the Name of God. This is supposed to be last work of the Guru at Kartarpur. It is a poem of spiritual love of God in which the Guru considers himself as the Bride of God. The poem describes the various changes through which a bride passes before the union takes place. The Karma (good or bad deeds) of life is main governing factor in human life. The poem contains seventeen stanzas. It begins with the month of Chait (March -April) and ends with Phagun (February-March).

Chait (Chait 1 = March 22)

It is the spring season when everything is green and flowers are blooming. The Almighty is everywhere in land, water and vegetation. The devotee who is meditating on His name wants to meet Him. I would fall on the feet of any one who would take me in this month to meet the Almighty. This is the beginning towards God realisation.

Vaisakh (Vaisakh 1 = April 21)

In the month of Vaisakh/Baisakh, trees are covered with green leaves, and the Guru (bride) stands at the door of her house to meet her husband (Almighty) The Guru says that in this world the relations of son and wife are temporary and worthless. The real and permanent relation is with the Almighty. Meditating on the name of God will bring happiness in this and the next world. The Guru is asking the Almighty to come to his house to make him happy. With God's name in heart and on tongue —the Guru looks very happy and charming.

Jeth (Jeth 1 = May 22)

Jeth/Jaistha. The weather is getting hot in the month. Bride (the Guru) suffers from loneliness and wishes to meet the Almighty. Meditating on God's name is such a priceless pearl that it cannot be taken by any one. A devotee's good Karma (good deeds), true devotion, virtue and love will take him/her near to the God.

Asarh (Asarh 1 = June 22)

Asarh/Ashad/Har is a very hot month and all the beings feel miserable due to heat in this month. Devotee wishes to see the Lord, if the devotee's mind is pure, virtuous, and full of love—Almighty will definitely meet the devotee. Only that person can be saved from the heat of Asarh, in whose heart dwells Almighty.

Savan (Savan 1 = July 22)

Savan/Sravan. In this month there is a lot of rain, and thunder and lightning in the sky frighten the bride (devotee). All those who minds are full of God's name will merge with the Lord. Devotee is feeling separated from God and will be happy when Lord merges in the heart of His devotee.

Bhadon (Bhadon 1 = August 23)

Bhadon/Bhadra. In this month there is water everywhere when all creatures are happy. A devotee can be united with the Lord if Guru's advice is followed. The Guru is the real saviour from destruction and hell.

Asu (Asu 1 = September 23)

Asu/Asvin/Asauj . In this month there are flowers and trees full of green leaves a sign of approaching winter. The Almighty can be reached through true love under the guidance of the Guru. All the happiness will be yours, once you are blessed by the love of God.

Katak (Katak 1 = Octobeer 23)

Katak/Kartak. The month of Katak has come and it reminds you that whatever has happened to you was due to your Karma (good or bad actions). If you remember His Name, the Lord will save you from destruction and evil things. One should always seek the guidance of a Guru and move in a holy company.

Maghar (Maghar 1 = November 23)

Maghar/Agrahayana/Mangsar. The message of this month is that those who move in a holy company, meditate on the name of God, and seek the guidance of the Guru are always happier and others are unhappy and miserable. Lord is the only helper and must offer your sincerest devotions to Him.

Poh (Poh 1 = December 22)

Poh/Pousa/Posh. It is very cold month in winter when trees have shed their leaves. The bride (devotee) has followed the instructions of the Guru. Devotee wants to unite with the God and liberate his soul from bondage. Dedicate your life in serving the Lord and you will be free from all sorrows.

Magh (Magh 1 = January 21)

The message of this month is that all sins can be washed if one keeps the company of holy men. One should listen to holy words and meditate on the name of God. Uniting with the Lord is like bathing in the Ganges, the Yamuna and at their confluence with Sarasvati. In this month meditating on the name of God is blissful like bathing at sixty-eight places of pilgrimage.

Phagun (Phagun 1 = February 20)

Phagun/Phalgun. In this month all those will be united with the Lord in whose heart the Guru had manifested Himself. The holy men guide those who wish to learn to reach God by meditating on His name. When one is united with the God, one gets complete joy and happiness. All the desires are fulfilled if one meditates on the name of God. The devotee thanks the Guru for showing the way to unite with God.

Gurmat

It means the Guru's teachings. It is not only a philosophy but also a way of life. Guru says that man is divine in origin, but man's ego is the wall between man and God. Man is body, mind and soul. His progress implies the balanced development of all parts. Body is the temple of God and has, therefore, to be cared for. The mind is to be illuminated with wisdom. The soul has to be nourished with the Holy Name.

Karma (law of action and reaction). The principle of Karma operates in physical, psychic and mental life. There are two kinds of actions: Good and Bad. Good actions (Bhakti, Karma, Adhatam Karma, and Hukam Razai Karma) are beneficial to yourself and every one around you.. Bad actions are harmful to you and to the society.

Five principles of dynamic living are: (1) honest labour, productivity not parasitism; (2) charity is duty, obligation and social welfare, and one must also share food and wealth with others, (3) Nam japna, remembering the name of god and living upto His qualities is essential, (4) It is essential to follow the Truth and one must not lie or be hypocrite. (5) Always keep a good company to learn good things. (6) Social commitment—always observe duties towards family, society, nation and humanity. One must always control over five vices (lust, anger, worldly attachment, greed and pride). (7) The true Sikh: a combination of Bhakti and Shakti. Blessed are those who repeats god's name and thinks of war against evil in mind. Sikhism is a faith of grace. Man may sow the seed and water the plant, but it may be washed away by flood. Prayer is a means of supplication and seeking Divine Grace.

Gurmataas

Literally it means the Guru's decision. It is an institution established by Guru Gobind Singh to ensure that all decisions and problems facing the community are taken by means of resolution passed by the Guru Panth. It is a form of the supreme authority of the collective will of the people duly formulated. It became the popular mode of taking decisions in the crisis facing the Sikhs in the eighteenth century. Decisions or Gurmataa's pertained to matters of foreign policy, the nature of military operations, the selection of commanders, the disputes between the Sikh chieftains and Misaldars, matters of propogation of Sikh faith and the management of Sikh shrines.

The conditions for the validity of a Gurmataa are:

1. It must be taken at any of the five Takhts in the presence of the Guru Granth Sahib.
2. The participants must forget their mutual differences and prejudices.

3. Panj Pyaras and Jathedar (leader) must be selected on the basis of merit and religious talents.
4. Gurmataa must be unanimous and decisions are unacceptable.
5. The subject of Gurmataa must be concerned with the welfare of the Sikh community and the country as a whole.
6. Every Sikh must obey Gurmataa and no one can undo or abrogate Gurmataa.

Regional Takhts take decisions on matters within their territorial jurisdiction. Gurmataa's are taken to clarify and support the fundamental principles of the Sikh faith, the Guru Granth Sahib, the purity of ritual and public organisation; questions of political, social and educational nature may be decided by it. Gurmataa's are different from Hukamnamas (proclamations issued by the Gurus and later by the Jathedar's of the Akal Takht). Ranjit Singh (Maharaja of Panjab) stopped political Gurmataas and it was started in 1920 when the Shiromani Gurdwara Prabandhak Committee and Shiromani Akali Dal were formed.

Hukamnama

It means the edicts or orders issued by the Sikh Gurus to individuals or Sangat. After the ten Gurus, the wives of Guru Gobind Singh and later Banda Bahadur issued Hukamnamas. Jathedars of the Akal Takht and the other four Takhts have issued and can issue Hukamnamas. A Hukamnama is an order binding on all Sikhs, and its rejection may lead to the punishment of the offender, and even ex-communication from the Sikh community. The first Hukamnama was issued by Guru Har Gobind (6th Guru) about his installation, the creation of Akal Takht. The Hukamnamas issued by the Gurus consist of missionary activities, for example, demands for money to run community kitchen, messages and ending of the Masand system (collection of money by Masands), and. during the

Misals period it was on the basis of Gurmata passed by the Sarbat Khalsa. For more information on Hukamnamas: see The Sikh World: an encyclopaedic survey of Sikh religion and culture by R.C. Dogra MBE and Urmila Dogra. New Delhi, UBSPD, 2003.

Gurus —their influence on Indian people

The Gurus left a great impact on Indian people by providing them leadership during the times of tyrannical Muslim rulers. Guru Nanak was a Hindu reformer of modern times who tried to emancipate the Hindu mind from the fetters of mythology. As it is mentioned in Vedic literature, Nanak declared that God alone to be worshipped in the spirit, and truth was greater than all religious rites and ceremonies. He was the first among the Hindus to raise his voice against tyranny and oppression of Muslims. He expressed strongly against the aggressive fanaticism of Islam, and expressed grief at the sufferings of the Hindus from Muslim rulers. He declared that Muslim rulers were butchers and darkness of falsehood was reigning supreme during Muslim rule.

Nanak became the Hero of every Hindu in the Panjab and tried to improve their spiritual and moral tone. Nanak's teachings were a great step towards arousing consciousness of a common nationality.

Hindus and some Muslims appreciated the guidance of Nanak and other Gurus in spiritual, moral, social, economic, cultural and political fields. During the Guru period the Hindus were suffering from the cruelty of Muslim rulers. They gave them hope of defending themselves from the cruelty of the rulers. They removed despair, false beliefs and fear from the minds of people by showing them the path of hope, confidence and peace.

Hindu and Muslim reformation

Guru Nanak's genius and spiritual illumination tried to root out the hatred between Hindus and Muslims. He declared there was only one God and preached the principal of fatherhood of God and brotherhood of man. Everybody was known as Bhai (brother) or Bebe (sister, mother or elderly woman). He told people that (a) Vedas, Puran and Quran taught love of humanity; (b) in the eyes of God every person (poor or rich) is equal; (c) taught people to discard rituals and surrender to Lord for peace of mind; (d) and stimulated the people against priesthood, caste system, polytheism and tyranny. He also preached them that their misfortunes were due to their misdeeds in the past life, and assured them that a good life would bring them salvation hereafter.

Muslims and Gurus

The Gurus tried to remove bitterness prevailing between Hindus and Muslims. Guru Nanak made Mardana his life long companion who was also the Guru's first Muslim disciple. His real name was Marjana (to die), and the Guru changed his name to Mardana (brave or manly). After Mardana's death his son Shahzada was employed to sing holy songs. Many other Muslim became the followers of Guru Nanak. Guru Angad employed two Muslim minstrels (Satta and Balwand) to sings sacred hymns at the time of worship. Guru Arjan got the foundation stone of Hari Mandar laid by a Muslim saint called Mian Mir of Lahore. To show friendship with Muslim he also included in the Adi Granth hymns of Muslim saints (Kabir, Farid, Mardana, Satta and Balwant.

Guru Hargobind employed in his service a large number of Pathans. At the battle of Bhaghani in 1688 Pir Buddhun Shah of Sadhaura gave to Guru Gobind 700 of his disciples in command of his four sons, two of whom were killed in the battle. In the battle of Anandpur in 1702 Mir Beg and Mamun Khan commanded Guru's forces. In 1704 General Saiyyid Beg did not like to fight an unholy war against the Guru and went over to his side. Nabi Khan and Ghani Khan of Machhiwara helped Guru Gobind in escaping towards Malwa desert. At that time Qazi Pir Muhammad saved Guru

Gobind's life by saying that he was a Muslim saint. Rai Kalia was also another Muslim devotee who brought the sad news of the murder of his little sons.

Music—Divine

Music in Hindu musical theory is regarded as a means to a definite emotional end of the many sounds which constitute the domain of music, human voice is the highest form, hence intoning, chanting, the recitation of mantras, Kirtan and singing, are regarded as the most effective means of expressing sound. The art of music was once known only in paradise. Indra had musicians in Svarga who excelled in various forms of this art. The Apsaras (heavenly nymphs) were devoted to the dance, the Kinnaras were instrumentalists, and the Gandarvas were celestial singers.

The elements of musical theory are first found in the Vedas, especially the Sama-Veda, whose chants were sung in a special manner. Music has been regarded as a sacred art. Sacred music was known as Marga Sangeet, while secular music was called Desi Sangeet. In India, the contributions of saints and seers to the development of classical music have been manifold and significant. Jaideva (1100 AD) of Gita Govinda was one of the first mystical singers of Vaishnavite Bhakti. His Geeta Govinda is regarded as a classic of devotional music. He sang the love of Lord Krishna and Radha with great emotion and sincerity. Chaitanya Mahaprabhu (1484-1534) of Bengal also sang the mystic love of Krishna and Radha. Swami Haridas (1480-1575), the teacher of Tansen was a great expert in the dhrupad style of devotional music. The first five Gurus (1469-1606) were also great singers and musicologists. They also encouraged professional singers for the benefit of their congregation. In 1604 the sacred hymns of the five Gurus, bards and saints were collected and named Adi Granth. The Gurus regarded sacred music as a means of spiritual uplift. The Granth is written wholly in verse and the hymns are not arranged in the holy book according to their authors, but according to thirty-one ragas or musical measures to which they were composed.

In India, the Bhakti (devotional worship) movement gave an impetus to sacred music. The following are nine traditional stages of Bhakti:

1. Sunan (hearing of the Holy Word).
2. Singing in praise of God Simran (remembrance of the Lord)
3. Puja (worship of the God)
4. Pad sevan (surrender at the Lord's feet
5. Vandhana (supplication to the Lord)
6. Dasa Bhava (Obeying the Lord as His servant)
7. Maitri Bhava (Total dependence on Lord as his companion)
8. Atam nivedan (Surrendering to God and merging the individual soul with the Universal Soul).

In Sikh devotional worship Kirtan is the devotional singing of the praises of God in melody and rhythm. The hymns are suing in classical raga with the appropriate tala. Guru Tegh Bahadur said that Kiran is the singing of the glory of God with words, mind and actions. Singing produces appropriate feeling and helps in the process of meditation. Guru Arjan Dev said that righteousness; wealth, success and salvation could be achieved by kirta.

Out of 1430 pages of the Guru Granth Sahib there are about 1343 pages, which are mostly in music. It shows the harmony between the Gurus and Raga. Like the ancient seers, the Gurus realised the power of music over mind and soul, and as such they conveyed their innermost feelings through the medium of music. The sacred music appeals to all men even though the meaning of the wording may be unintelligible to some. People consider it a song, but in fact it is a meditation on Divinity.

Sikh mode of address
Sat Sri Akal

Truth is timeless or immortal Lord or God is the only truth.. This is the Sikh greeting. This saying is the second part of the Jaikara (Jo Bole So Nihal, Sat Sri Akal) (He who says this is blessed: God is the only Truth or Truth is immortal Lord)

Wah Guru

The proper exclamation of community of faith of the Sikh as a sect is simply (Wah Guru—meaning, O Guru or Hail Guru.) The lengthened exclamation of the Sikh greeting was prescribed by Guru Gobind Singh for all Sikhs was (Wahe Guru Ji Ka Khalsa, Wahe Guru Ji Ki Fatah, meaning that Khalsa (pure) belongs to God and as such victory also belongs to God.

Jo bole so nihal sat sri akal. It is a traditional Sikh saying, which means: He who says this is saved: Truth is the immortal Lord. (He who says that truth/honesty is the immortal Lord. is blessed by God or saved by God).

Sardar. In Sikh culture the word Sardar is equivalent to Mr. or Esquire. A married Sikh woman is called a Sardarni. When a man does not know the name of a Sikh, he is usually addressed as Sardar Ji or Sardar Sahib or his wife Sardarni Ji or Sardarni Sahiba or Bahen Ji or Mata Ji These modes of addresses are current in upper classes. Amongst the peasantry a man is referred to as Bhai Ji or Bhai Sahib (brother) or woman as Bahen Ji or Bibi Ji (sister). Amongst the aristocrats the head of the family is addressed as Raja Sahib and his wife as Rani Sahiba. The elder son is addressed as Tikka Sahib and his wife as Tikka Rani; and the young sons as Kunwars and their wives as Kunwar Ranis. Some professional titles attached to the names are: Gyani (scholar), Akali (political party).

Chardian Kalan/Chardi Kala

It is a state of mind, which is cheerful in sorrow and

suffering and stoically optimistic even in the face of a hopelessly critical situation. Having confidence in the ultimate justice neither of God, the Sikh neither surrenders to despair nor to the terror of oppression. It is also an outlook of dynamic optimism.

Ik Omkar

Ik Omkar is the first word in the Guru Granth Sahib, used by Guru Nanak in the Japji. It means One God, One Supreme Reality. The first line in the Holy book is: Ik Omkar, Satnam Karta Purakh, Nirbhau Nirvair, Akalmurti, Ajuni, Saibhang, Gurprasad. (It means that there is only one God, God is truth, He is the Creator, God is without fear, He is without animosity. He is the immortal Being. He is Unborn, He is self-existent. God is realised by the grace of Guru).

Many of the chapters of the books into which the Guru Granth Sahib is divided, begin with the expression Iko Omkar or Eko Omkar, Sat Guru Prasad (meaning The One God, and the grace of the blessed Guru).

Guru. In Sikhism Guru stands for God, for example, God was the Guru of Nanak.

Tradition of Sikh Gurus on women

Guru Nanak on women

Nanak himself had not repudiated women, and appreciated the life of a household. He had a wife and family and his life separate from them had not been absolute. Gobind Singh (10th Guru) had more than one wife. In any case, Sikhs were working out their own peculiar ideas of womanhood, which differed from the Muslim viewpoint.

Guru Nanak had two sons, but one of them was dissolute. The other Sri Chand, had given his father only a qualified devotion. But his mother was insistent that the choice should fall, nevertheless on him. Nanak selected Angad his successor in preference to either of his sons. Angad was confirmed as the second Guru by many signs, including an appearance of the Goddess Durga. Nanak himself retired to Kartarpur, a village near Ravi, to end his days, leaving Angad to carry the umbrella of spiritual authority over his followers.

In his poem Barah Mah the figure of the young and most beautiful bride depicts the most vivid images, and portrays the human relationship with the Divine. The individual is represented as bride who is seeking union with her groom (Divine).

The poem Bara Mah is supposed to be the last work of the Guru at Kartarpur. It is a poem of spiritual love of God in which the Guru considers himself as the Bride of God. The poem depicts the various changes through which a bride passes before the union takes place. The Karma (good or bad deeds) of life is the main governing factor in human life. The poem contains seventeen stanzas. It begins with the month of Chait (March-April) and ends with Phagun (February-March). The holy men guide those who wish to learn to reach God by meditating on His name. When one is united with the God, one gains complete joy and happiness. All the desires are fulfilled if one meditates on the name of God.

Guru Nanak tells us that in his days the Kings had become butchers and cannibals, official dogs licked the blood and devoured the flesh of the people in their power; there was none to protect the honour of the weak, Hindus and women. All was falsehood, and religion had flown away from horrors as it beheld when Babar came to India. Most people sunk under the burden of misery into a pessimistic resignation, but it stung Nanak into even challenging God for tolerating such brutalities (Asa Ki war 39: 1-2).

Guru Nanak emphasised the equality of all human beings and gave woman a status and role in society equal to that of man. In the Guru Granth Sahib the Guru said why do you call woman bad, for she gives birth to great men as well as kings.

From the woman is our birth; in the woman's womb are we shaped.

To the woman are we engaged; to the woman are we wedded.
The woman is our friend, and from the woman is the family.
If one woman dies, we seek another; through the woman are the bonds of the world.
Why call woman evil who gives birth to kings and all?
From the woman is the woman; without the woman there is none.
Nanak: Without the woman is the One True Lord alone. (GGS p.473)

In Sri Rag ki Var Guru Nanak says that perfect shall obtain a sight of God; the fool shall find no place with Him. Here the Guru mentions the women's duty:

If women adorn themselves with love and affection for their Spouse (God),
They shall not be restrained from their devotion to Him (God) day or night.
They shall abide in His (God) chambers, and the Word shall regenerate them;
They shall humbly supplicate the True One;
And they shall appear beautiful near their Spouse (God) walking according to His (God) order;
They shall make hearty supplication to the Beloved.
Accursed the homes, wretched the lives of those who possess not the word.
They whose hopes are fulfilled by the Word quaff nectar.

In Majh ki Var—Guru Nanak says about a woman's happy married life:

In the house where the Beloved celebrated His marriage
Female friends sang songs of rejoicing,

Where the Spouse hath adorned the bride, there reign joy and pleasure.
The woman who is dear to her husband, is beautiful, clever, skilful,
Well conducted, and distinguished:
She is accomplished, and very fortunate;
She possesseth sons and is a virtuous wife;
She hath all decorations, and it is she who is wise.
She who is adorned with the love of her Spouse, is of good family and a queen.
The greatness of her whom her Spouse hath embraced cannot be described.
The married life of her who hath the support of the love of the unapproachable and inapprehensible spouse shall be eternal.

Guru Amar Das (3rd Guru) on women

As a regular visitor to Haridwar, the Guru noticed that the Pandas had divided their own areas of operation to collect offerings. The Guru adopted the same device and divided his area of operation into 22 branches called Manjis (missionary assignment). Manji means a cot, and the representative of the Guru would sit on it and collect offerings for Langar (communal kitchen) on Baisakhi, Diwali or other special occasions. Sometimes a priest would sit on it and deliver his sermon or lead the congregation into singing hymns from the holy book of the Sikhs. The Guru treated men and women equally and appointed two women as head of Manji (missionary assignment). Mai Bhago at village Wayun, Rupar district and Mai Sewan at village Gardnoh in Patiala district. Until this Guru's time the Guruship was not given to his own family member, but he made it hereditary as he was highly pleased with the single-minded devotion and service of his daughter Bhani and son-in-law Ram Das, a Sodhi Khatri of Lahore.

Guru Ramdas (4th Guru) on women

Guru Ramdas composed Lavan, a composition of four verses in Guru Granth Sahib in Rag Suhi on page 773. It was composed as a wedding song for the Sikhs. These verses are recited twice, first by the Granthi, and sung when the bride and groom go around the Holy Granth. The purpose of repetition is to stress the spiritual goal as mentioned in the Lavan. It promotes the spirit of resignation to the Will of God and builds up one's patience. These verses indicate the values and virtues of the ideal married life, as a journey towards perfection.

The freedom of women and their emancipation from the tyranny of the parda (veil) may be inferred from the manner in which Bhai Budha received Mata Ganga the wife of Guru Arjan, from Guru Amar Das's refusal to receive a Rani (queen) who had visited him when she was closely veiled, and from Kabir's address to his daughter-in-law. The word Mata (mother) is a Sanskrit word and Hindus and Sikhs give the title Mata (mother) to the wives of the Gurus, in the same way as they gave the title Baba or father to Guru Nanak.

Guru Arjan Dev (5th Guru) on women

In the hymns of Guru Arjan Dev—holiness is described under the allegory of a perfect woman:

A house is adorned by the presence of a woman who is virtuous and devotion incarnate,
Whose beauty is incomparable, and conduct without reproach.
Some rare holy man may find her;
On meeting the Guru I have found such a well-behaved woman:
She shedeth lustre on feasts and marriages.
As long as she lived without father (spiritual ignorance),
Her husband, wandered about very lonely,
When I served and conciliated the true man,

He brought her to my house, and I obtained all happiness.
She possesseth the thirty-two good qualities; true and holy are her offspring;
She is obedient, accomplished, and beautiful,
She fulfilleth the wishes of her husband and her lord;
She comforteth in every way her husband's younger and elder brothers' wives;

She is best of the household; She gives counsels to her husband's younger and elder brothers.

Best is the home in which she hath appeared.
Nanak, its inmates pass their time in perfect t happiness

Gobind Singh (10th Guru) on women

Forty Sikh soldiers who were with Guru Gobind Singh in the besieged Anandpur fort in 1704 could not bear the hardships and starvation. They left the Guru and returned to their homes. When they reached their homes they were criticised by their wives for leaving the Guru at the time when he needed them most. The deserters realised their mistake and decided to return to the Guru's camp under the leadership of Mai Bhago, a woman warrior. After reaching the Guru's camp they fought with the Mughal army and all of them died except one Sardar Mahan Singh. The Guru blessed the forty martyrs and performed their last rites. Mata Sundari, Guru Gobind Singh widow, issued Hukam Namas (orders), which were binding to all Sikhs.

In his Dasama Granth the most invincible woman is Goddess Durga who captured the attention of the last Guru. The opening verse from Chandi Charitra (wonder of Chandi or the Goddess) in which goddess Durga is identified with the sword, forms part of the Sikh supplicatory prayer to this day. There are two portions called Chandi Charitra of which this is considered the greater. It relates the destruction of eight Titans or Deityas by Chandi the Goddess. It occupies 20 pages, and it is understood to be a translation of a Sanskrit legend, executed by Gobind himself. It is the same legend as the greater Chandi in a different metre. It occupies about 15 pages. A supplement to the legends of Chandi called Chandi ki Var occupies about six pages.

Another work of the last Guru is called Istri Charitra (tales of women). There are 404 stories, illustrative of the character and disposition of women. A stepmother became enamoured of her stepson, the heir of a monarchy, who would not gratify her desires, whereupon she represented to her husband that his first-born had made attempts upon her honour. The Raja ordered his son to be put to death, but his ministers interfered, and procured a respite. They then enlarged in a series of stories upon the nature of women, and at length the Raja became sensible of the guilt of his wife's mind, and of his own rashness. These stories occupy 446 pages, or nearly half of the Granth. The name of Sham also occurs as the writer of one or more of them.

The Gurus liberated women rejected the practice of isolation of widows, sati system, and bride price and female infanticide. As it is mentioned in Vedic literature the Gurus similarly instructed their followers to regard women as either mothers, sisters and daughters, depending on their age.

Wives of Gurus and their contribution to the society

During the Guru's time the position of a wife was one of greater honour, for she shared with her husband the performance of duties, as it is known during the Vedic age. She was the mistress of the house (griha patni), with control not only over servants, but also over the unmarried brothers and sisters of her husband. As the family could only be continued in the male line, prayers for the abundance of sons are very frequent. As we know that the wife of the fifth Guru went to Bhai Buddha for his blessings to have a son. The birth of a daughter was also welcomed. The wedding was celebrated in the house of the bride's parents, to which the bridegroom came in procession with his relations and friends. Here they were entertained with many preparations from cow's milk and vegetarian meals. Here, too, the future husband, taking the bride's hand, led her round the nuptial fire, later the Guru Granth Sahib. Then the bride, anointed and in festal attire, mounted with her husband a cart, which was adorned with red flowers and drawn by two bulls. If the cart was not available the bride would sit in a Palki (sedan) and depart.

Women have in Sikhism, from the time of the Gurus, a status comparable with that of men. When Guru Nanak left home and started his missionary activities, Nanaki the elder sister of Guru Nanak, bought Rabab (musical instrument) for Mardana and also helped financially her brother's family. She also advised Maradana to stay with Guru Nanak for his salvation. The role of Mata Sulakhni (wife of Guru Nanak) is unique. She looked after her children alone, maintained her grace, dignity, self-reliance, sacrificed her personal comfort for the mission of her husband, and did not feel depressed when she had to live away from her husband. Guru Angad started a free kitchen and his wife (Mata Khiwi) used to manage it. In the kitchen she maintained a feeling of equality and asked every one to sit together without any distinction of caste or status.

Mata Mansa Devi (wife of Guru Amardas) was not only the mistress of the house but also helped the Guru in his religious activities. The daughter of Guru Amardas (Bhani Devi), wife of Guru Ramdas and mother of Guru Arjan Dev looked after the religious activities of his father. Prithvi Chand, the eldest son of the Guru, wanted to become the Guru, but she helped her younger son (Guru Arjan Dev) to become the fifth Guru. When Arjan Dev was arrested by the King (Jahangir), she maintained her patience and did not even allow her daughter-in-law (Ganga Devi) to loose heart and instead prepared her for the martyrdom of her husband.

Mata Ganga (wife of Guru Arjan Dev and mother of Guru Har Gobind) gave birth to her only son after many years of her marriage. On the request of her husband she went to

Baba Buddha for blessing, and gave birth to a great warrior son (6th Guru).

Mata Nanaki, wife of Guru Hargobind, and the mother of Guru Tegh Bahadur (9th Guru) had to go through hard times as the sixth Guru fought wars with the Mughals. After the Guru's death she isolated herself, in order to save herself, from family quarrels of succession to Guruship.

Mata Kishan Devi, wife of Guru Har Rai was the mother of Guru Har Krishan. She used to manage the affairs of the Gurdwara. She never displeased her son (8th child Guru) and helped him to run the affairs of his religious duties. Mata Gujari was the wife of the ninth Guru and mother of the tenth and last Guru. Mata Gujari witnessed the martyrdom of her husband and the sacrifice of her grandsons. She taught her son and grandsons Sikh Dharama and righteousness.

Guru Gobind Singh had three wives (Mata Sundari, Jito and Sahib Devan). Mata Sundari lived for about 40 years after the Guru's death, issued about nine Hukam Namas and became leader of the Khalsa. Mata Sahib Devan took Amrit and was proclaimed as the mother of Khalsa. She always helped Mata Sundari in social and religious affairs, and issued about nine Hukam Namas. There is very little known about Mata Jito except that she was the mother of the Guru's youngest son (Fateh Singh) born at Anandpur in 1698. Gobind's own wife, it may be recalled, took part in the formation of the Khalsa and threw Patasa (small sugar cakes) into the baptismal bowl of Amrit, at the first initiation ceremony, in order that the Khalsa and its orders might be sweetened. Women as well as men received baptism (Pahul), and did the same duties as men. Women worshipped with the men in the temples and Gurdwaras, and never wore a veil. The freedom among the women of the Sikhs is exhibited in the very form of marriage, in which women's rights were publicly acknowledged like the Hindus. Anand form of marriage came to be recognised by the Panjab Government in1909.

3

Customs, Manners and Beliefs

Akhand Path

It means continuous reading of Adi Granth/Guru Granth Sahib by a relay of readers. This generally takes 48 hours. The reading must never be interrupted. It can be held on either occasions of joy or sorrow. It is said that this practice began in the eighteenth century when the Sikhs had to stay away in jungles and isolated places in order to avoid the persecution of Muslim rulers. Both men and women can participate in the Akhand Path. If the Akhand Path is held in a house, the family listens to the Akhand Path and also look after the comfort of readers by providing them vegetarian food and rest. The reader is expected to take a bath and wear clean clothes before taking his turn for the recitation. In Gurdwara Hazur Sahib at Nander, Akhand Path of the Dasam Granth is also held from time to time, but it is not customary to have Akhand Path of Dasam Granth in Gurdwaras or in homes The Sikh Rahat Maryada published by the SGPC, Amritsar, lays down the guidelines for the ceremony of Akhand Path of Adi Granth/ Guru Granth Sahib.

Arati

Arati word is originated from Sanskrit aratrika, meaning the light. Usually on a plate of copper, a lamp made of rice-flour, earth or some metal is placed. It is supplied with ghee (melted butter), or oil and lighted. Usually women and sometime men take hold of the plate, and raising as high as the person or idol, for whom the ceremony is performed, describe in that position a number of circles with the plate and the burning lamp. The intention of this ceremony with humans is to keep away from them the evil influence of malevolent or jealous looks. When influence person (King, princes etc.) appear in public, the first thing that is done on their return home, is to perform this ceremony of Arti, as an antidote to the ill-designed looks which may have been cast upon them. The Arti was also performed in olden days when heroes used to return home victorious. The Arti at the Puja ceremony (worship) is performed daily in the morning and evening at Hindu and Jain temples. It is a part of worship to perform Arti in front of the deity for blessings of good health, prosperity and peace in the world. The Arti ceremony in variant forms is also observed in other countries of the world.

Arti is also performed in some Sikh temples in front of the Adi Granth, as a concluding ceremony for an Akhand-Path (unbroken reading of the holy book from beginning to end), and also at the close of the evening service at a Gurdwara.)

Meditation on God's name, by conquering passion, anger, greed, ego, devotion to Guru, surrendering to God etc. Bards claim to be the ocean of knowledge, teaching three R's and committing to memory the pedigrees of their patrons.

Ik Omkar, Satnam Karta Purakh, Nirbhau Nirvair, Akalmurti, Ajuni, Saibhang, Gurprasad.

There is only one God, God is truth, He is the Creator, God is without fear, He is without animosity, He is the immortal being. He is unborn. He is self-existent, God is realised by the grace of the Guru.

Bards to inspire religious and just warfare

Hymns of the bards (Bhatt bani) about 20 pages are included in the concluding part of the Guru Granth Sahib. At that time it was the custom to recite on the eve of the battle the praises and warlike deeds of Hindu ancestors, for the purpose of inciting to bravery, dispelling cowardice, and filling the hearts of troops with valour to defend their faith. Thus Guru Gobind Singh maintained fifty-two bards to translated the Mahabhatata, the Ramayan, and the gallant achievements of Ram, Krishna, goddess Chandi and others. He translated tenth canto of the Bhagawat Puran, in which he recounts chivalrous exploits of Krishna (in which he inculcate the doctrine of Bhakti (faith) and duty of a soldier). This was to inspire ardour for religious and just warfare as taught by Lord Krishna in Mahabharata.

The tenth Guru also translated the praises of goddess Chandi, a poem of 700 verses, forming an episode of the Markandeya Puran. It celebrates Durga's victories over the Asuras (demons), and is read daily in the temples of that goddess. He himself translated so that they might be chanted for warlike purposes, and even cowards on hearing her story might obtain courage and the hearts of the brave beat with fourfold enthusiasm. Many of the bards employed by Guru Gobind Singh were enlisted in the army of the Guru and were killed by the army of Aurangzeb.

Kalsahar was a great composer of hymns who wrote in praise of the first five Gurus, and the rest of the bards also wrote in praise of one or the other Guru.

All the bards (Bhatt) were Vaishnava devotees of Lord Ram and Krishna, and in their adorations of the Gurus they spoke in the languages of their Hindu Vaishnava traditions. A Bhatt would always remember by heart, and repeat from memory offhand, the verses they have compiled in praise of the Gurus or the pedigrees of the head of families within the tribe. They believed that whoever will become Guru would inherit all the good qualities of the earlier Gurus. They believed that all the Gurus were incarnation of Guru Nanak, they attained the height of spiritual glory through fulfil all the duties of domestic and social life, but let not your heart forget your spiritual nature.

Discipline—Sikhism

It is customary to maintain discipline. A Sikh or a devotee must begin by keeping the company of good people (Sadh-sangat) and cultivate purity of character. The character supplies the soil for the sowing of the seed which is meditation on the name (Nam and Gian) is the fruit of virtuous character. Discipline means total subjugation of the lower instinct of lust, anger, blind attachment, covetousness, vanity; and development of the higher virtues, such as the proper use of the bodily essence, contentment, kindness to all forms of life, faith in divine existence, purity of body and mind, charity and benevolence, toleration, and thoughtfulness. To discipline his mind one must always keep the company of holy men and learn to live independently by earning an honest livelihood. True discipline is cultivated not by living in seclusion but by leading a life useful in all respects.

Five Ks (Panj Kakkas)

Guru Gobind Singh modified the Sikh Baptism ceremony when he created the Khalsa in 1699. This ceremony was called Amrit (baptism), when Amrit (nectar) is stirred by the double-edged sword (Khande-de-pahul). The recipients are asked to take certain vows and abide by the code of discipline (rahat) and keep the five Ks or Kakkas. They are called the five Ks/ Kakkas because their names begin with the letter K. The five Ks/Kkkas are as under:

1. Kes or unshorn hair. Guru Nanak had started the practice of maintaining hair on the body. It was a symbol of harmony with the will of God. Hair is an integral part of the human body which ensures proper health and hygiene for it has to be kept clean and uncut
2. Kanga (comb) is necessary to keep hair neat and tidy. The

hair on the head should be tied into a knot and covered with a neat turban.

3. Kara (steel wrist band) symbolised restraint from evil action. After wearing Kara one takes a vow that he/she will never do anything evil.
4. Kachh (underpants) should be worn at all times. It ensures briskness of action and freedom of movement. It also symbolise control over passion or sex.
5. Kirpan (sword). It is an emblem of courage and is meant both for protection of the weak and the poor, and also for self-defence. It promotes martial spirit and willingness to sacrifice oneself for the defence of truth, justice and moral values.

The Five Ks along with turban are the Khalsa uniform for promoting the solidarity and identity of the community. They keep the Sikhs united in the pursuit of ideas and vows made to the Guru.

Karam

It means action, work (an act of piety or religion), duty or acts obligatory on an individual. All the object forms are the product of Karma. Suffering and happiness are the results of Karma. Karma stands for destiny, consequent upon your deeds or actions. In Sikhism the word Karma has a meaning different from its connotation in Hinduism. According to Hindu belief even good actions will not wipe out previous Karma until all the bad Karma is exhausted by good Karma, but Sikhism declaresd that God's grace can cut through the chain of transmigration and bring about man's salvation. According to Sikhism, Karma can be changed by prayer and Divine Grace. If a man submits to the will of God, he acts as his instrument and as such he is free from Karma. Past bad Karma can be erased through association with the holy and the virtuous, and by seeking the grace of God through meditation.

Khanda

In order to maintain Sikh customs Khanda is mainly used as a symbol. Khanda is the supreme insignia of the Khalsa. It consists of four concentric circles. Each of the three weapons, which make up the Khanda, has a symbolic meaning.

(1) The inner circle (Chakra), an ancient Hindu symbol, represents oneness of God./Waheguru, without beginning and without end, and the unity of humanity on equal terms.

(2) The two swords (Kirpans), one on either sides extend to the right and left of it, represent the spiritual power of Piri, and temporal power that is Miri. Such two swords were first worn by the Sixth Guru, Hargobind.

(3) The double-edged sword (Khanda) in the centre symbolises the ideal of the saint-soldier. The blades of the sword must be equally honed, otherwise its balance is lost and becomes useless. Khanda also represents the three forms of God –The Transcendent (Nirgun), the related (Sargun) and the Holy Name (Waheguru). The Khanda also represents the essence of Sikh philosophy—the uniqueness of God, the uniqueness of the twin ideals of Miri and Piri (saint-soldier), and the goal of salvation while alive. It is with Khanda (double edged sword) that the amrit is prepared for baptising the Khalsa.

According to Lou Singh, the two sword handles can be picked by any seeker of truth to become a saint-soldier, and be free from worldly temptations to reach the summit – saintliness and the Divine Court.

Khanda symbol can be seen on the flag of the Gurdwara, the Palki above the Guru Granth Sahib and on some ties and back of the body-warmers.

Meditation—Sikhism

It is customary to meditate on the name of god, who wishes to benefit by meditating or repeating (Nam Simran) the divine Name. When the character building of a devotee is complete, the devotee is initiated into the society of the pure. He is baptised by the five chosen and taught the method of meditation on the true name (Satnam). The message communicated to him at the Amrita ceremony—runs: 'henceforth you belong to the community of the Khalsa, your father is Sri Guru Gobind Singh (protector of the universe), your mother Sahib Devi (the supreme power), your abode Anandpu4r (city of bliss), your caste Sodh-bans (the family of the Lord). Your will be bound to wear five distinctive symbols:

(i) The Keshas, to preserve your brain in the normal condition. This is the sign of Yogi, implying abhorrence of all artificialities due to the desire to appear beautiful;
(ii) Kachch, meant to teach you the habit of using the life-fluid p roperly;
(iii) Kirpan, to teach you the necessity of cultivating physical development and warn you against the danger of bodily deterioration;
(iv) Kara to bind you to obedience of the Guru's law as given in the Holy Granth;
(v) Kangha, as the comb keeps the hair pure, even so twice a day you should try to purge away all filthy thoughts from your mind.

You should also recite five banis every day:-

(i) Jap Ji—comprising the main principles of Sikh spiritualism, ethics and divinity;
(ii) Jap—Giving the attributes of God, personal and impersonal;
(iii) Swsayas—inculcating the transistorises of material enjoyments and emphasising the brevity of human life;
(iv) Rahiras—the prayer for peace;
(v) Sohala—praise of the Divine.

You shall believe in the Gurus as the 10 manifestations of one and the same Lord, and obey the commandments given in the Holy Granth.

You will have to meditate on the holy name with full concentration of mind every day in the early morning.

You must perform all ceremonies (sanskaras) according the instructions of the Guru.

Methods of meditation.

In the first stage attention must be fixed on the personality of the Guru by reading his life and by constantly thinking of the attributes to be cultivated. Afterwards, silent repetition of the name together with the understanding of the sense in the mind. By constant practice the name itself vanishes and the spirit makes itself manifest in the devotee's heart according to his conception.

Ultimately the individual soul enjoys perfect union with the supreme soul. In this stage the Bhagat (devotee) see the one God within, without and everywhere and realises that: 'In Him he lives, moves and has his being.'

The Sikh believes that the Supreme Soul has fully manifested itself in the Guru. He is therefore, the creator, preserver; and it is he who is the destroyer of the universe.

Principles, beliefs and customs in Sikhism

1. *God—the Godhead*

The True Name is God; without fear, without enmity; the Being without Death, the Giver of Salvation; the Guru and Grace. Remembers the primal Truth; Truth, which was before the world, began:

By reflection it cannot be understood, if times innumerable
it be considered.
By meditation it cannot be attained, how much so ever the
attention be fixed.
A hundred wisdoms, even a hundred thousand, not one

accompanies the dead.
How can Truth be told, how can falsehood be unravelled?
O Nanak! By following the will of God, as by Him ordained.
(Nanak, Adi Granth, Japji (commencement of)
My mind dwells Upon One,
He who gave the Soul and the body (Guru Arjan, Adi Granth, Sri Rag)

2. Incarnations, saints and prophets.

Numerous Muhammads have there been, and multitudes of Brahmas, Vishnus, and Shivas, Thousands of Pirs and Prophets, and tens of thousands of saints and holy men, but the Chief of Lords is the One Lord, the true Name of God. (Nanak, Ratan Mala)

It should be noted that Hindus believe in One God, the ultimate reality called Brahman/Brahmin, which is the uncaused cause of this universe. Nothing exists without It. Brahman/Bramin is meditated upon in the neuter form and is regarded as uncreated, eternal, omnipotent, omnipresent, omniscient, transcendental, immanent. Other divinities are only manifestations of the same absolute Brahman/Brahmin, and derive their power and glory from Brahman/Brahmin (One God). Ekam sada vipra bahaudha vadanti (there is one Truth). The Hindu sages and other religions call it by different names. In Hinduism the one God cannot be divided but one can call It by different names.

3. The Sikh Gurus not to be worshipped

Idolatry is alien to the Sikh Gurus and during Vedic times, but pictures of Gurus are used as a focus of attention when praying; these may be garlanded with flowers, and Agarbatis (joss sticks) are sometimes burnt before them, though these things are not allowed in Sikhism.

In Visitor Natal Guru Gobind Singh says:
He who speaks of me as the Lord,
Him will I sink into the pit of Hell!

Consider me as the slave of God:
Of that have no doubt in thy mind.
I am but the slave of the Lord,
Come to behold the wonder of Creation.

4. Images and the worship of saints

In Sorath Rag (Adi Granth) Guru Nanak says:
Worship not another than God; bow not to the dead.

To worship an image, to make pilgrimage to a shrine, to remain in a desert and yet to have the mind impure, is all in vain, and thus thou can not be accepted. To be saved thou must worship Truth (God). God is worshipped, that by salvation may be attained.

Fall at the feet of God; in senseless stone God is not. (Gobind, Vichitr Natak).

In Vedas there is only one God and in Hinduism this God cannot be divided, but you can call it by different names.

5.Karma

It means action, work; an act of piety or of religion, duty or acts obligatory on an individual. All the object forms are the product of Karma. Suffering and happiness are the results of Karma (actions, deeds). Karma stands for destiny, consequent upon the deeds of previous births. This cumulative destiny is also known as Kirat. Karma is the result of actions, or the adjustment of the effects of actions. Bhakti (devotion of God) has a neutralizing effect on Karma. It is the law of action and reaction: as you sow, so shall you reap. Also the law of retribution. According to Hindu belief even good actions will not wipe out previous bad Karma (actions), until all the Karma is exhausted, but Sikhism declares that God's grace can cut through the chain of transmigration and bring about man's salvation. According to Sikhism, prayer and Divine Grace can change Karma. If a man submits to the Divine will, he acts as His instrument and as such he is free from Karma. Past Karma can be erased through association with the holy and the virtuous, and seeking the Grace of God through meditation.

6. Miracles

Guru Nanak did not believe in miracles. He did not believe in Sidhi (changer of shapes) or Ridhi (giver of never ending stores of richness). Guru Nanak in Adi Granth, Majh ki Var says:

Dwell thou in flames uninjured,
Remain unharmed amid ice eternal; Make blocks of stone thy daily food,
Spurn the Earth before thee with thy foot,
Weigh the Heavens in a balance;
And then ask of me to perform miracles.
Guru Nanak did not believe in these things.

7. Transmigration

Life is like the wheel circling on its pivot,
O Nanak! Of going and coming there is no end.

He who knows not the One God
Will be born again times innumerable. (Gobind, Midhi Mir.)

8. Faith

Eat and clothe thyself, and thou may'st be happy;
But without fear and faith there is no salvation.
(Guru Nanak, Adi Granth, Sohila Maru Rag).

9. Grace

O Nanak! He, on whom God looks, finds the Lord.
(Guru Nanak, Adi Granth, Asa Rag.)
O Nanak! He, on whom God looks, will fix his mind on the Lord.
Amar Das, Adi Granth, Bilawal.

10. Predestination

According to the fate of each, dependent on his actions, are his coming and going determined. This is the Law of Karma (deeds, actions) of Hindus.

(Guru Nanak, Adi Granth Asa ki Var)

11. Asceticism

A householder who does no evil,
Who is ever intent upon good,
Who continually exercised charity,
Such a householder is pure as the Ganges
(Guru Nanak, Adi Granth, Ram Kali Ragni)

12. Caste

Guru Nanak said in Adi Granth, Parbhati Ragni, that God will not ask him of his birth but he will ask what has he done.

Guru Amar Das in Adi Granth, Rag Bhairav says:

All says that there are four races,
But all are the seed of Brahm,
The world is but clay,
And of similar clay many pots are made.
Nanak says man will be judged by his actions,
And that without finding God there will be no salvation.
The body of man is composed of the five elements;
Who can say that one is high and another low?

All the Gurus were Khatris and they denounced the caste system, but due to unknown reasons they married their children in their own caste. The Gurus opposed caste from religious point of view, or creating distinction between different castes, but accepted caste to some extent from social point of view.

Most of the Sikhs still use caste names as surname, and some use Singh as a surname. Marriages customs are the same as the Hindus and are usually arranged within the community e.g. a Ramgarhia would usually marry within Ramgarhia community, a Jat within the Jat community and Kshatriya within their own community.

In India and abroad many Sikh temples are based on caste: Ramgarhia Gurdwara, Singh Sabha Gurdwara, Nirankari Gurdwara, Ravi Dasi Gurdwara, Kukas or Namdhari etc. Caste still exists among the Sikhs despite its rejection by the Gurus and Sikh Rahit Maryada (code of conduct). Among the Hindus and the Sikhs a man's caste is determined by his/her birth in the family. A child born in a Ramgarhia family will be called Ramgarhia, or a Jat or a Kshatriya etc. The constitution of India rejects the caste system. It has declared the practice of untouchability/unsociability as a criminal offence Usually Indian living abroad denies the caste system, but still it is being practised in India and abroad.

A Sikh would not marry within the same got or gotra (lineage, pedigree or exogamous caste grouping within a zat). Zat and got are regarded essential for marriages. All the Hindu customs are adopted for marrying within the same zat (caste), e.g. Kshatriya with the Kshatriya and Ramgarhiya with the Ramgarhiya or a Jat with a Jat. They are not allowed to marry within the same got (caste grouping or lineage).

Sikh code of conduct says that a Sikh should have only one wife, but Guru Hargobind and Guru Gobind Singh both had three wives each. Maharaja Ranjit Singh had several wives. In those days rich and influential people had more than one wife due to Muslim influence. Sikhism believes in monogamy, but some Jats in rural Panjab practice polygamy and also some poor Sikhs practice polyandry in order to prevent the land to be divided into small holdings. Divorce is not allowed in Hinduism and Sikhism, but it is happening if the marriage breaks down.

13. Food

Guru Nanak did not like the killing of animals for food. Guru Nanak in Adi Granth, Maj ki Var says that an animal slain without cause cannot be proper food. Any swacrifice which gives pain is not right.

Steel, devotion to steel is customary

Throughout India the implements of any calling are in a manner worshipped, or, in Western moderation of phrase, they are blessed or consecrated. This is especially noticeable among merchants, who annually perform religious ceremonies before a heap of gold; among hereditary clerks or writers, who similarly idolize their inkhorn; and among soldiers and military leaders, who on the Dussehra festival consecrate their banners and piled-up weapons. Guru Gobind withdrew his followers from that undivided attention which their fathers had given to the plough, the loom, and the pen, and he urged them to regard the sword as their principal stay in this world. The sentiment of veneration for that, which gives us power, or safety, or our daily bread, may be traced in all countries. It is this spirit, which must devote its energies to the service and contemplation of steel, while the increate soul contemplates God. Compare also the medieval ceremony of "watching his arms" regularly undergone by the candidate for knighthood.

The Scriptures – belief in scriptures

Adi Granth/Guru Granth Sahib and its contributors

It is customary for every Sikh and many Hindus to keep the holy book (Guru Granth Sahib/Adi Granth) in one room of their home, where the family can worship daily. The holy book in the home brings good luck, health, wealth and prosperity. The holy book is known to Hindus and Sikhs alike, but there are not many who understand the nature of its contents. The Adi Granth is written in Gurmukhi characters, but a small collection of its contents is in the Panjabi language. The best-known Panjabi portion is the Japji, the composition of Guru Nanak. Most of the contributors to the Guru Granth Sahib wrote in some form of Western Hindi, while others wrote in Marathi. Some portions, especially of the last section, are composed in Sanskrit. The Granth usually forms a quarto volume of about 1430 pages, each page containing about 27 lines, and each line containing about 35 letters.

The Adi Granth (the first book)/Guru Granth Sahib comprises:

(a) The writings attributed to Nanak, and the succeeding

teachers of the Sikh faith up to the ninth Guru (Tegh Bahadur), omitting the sixth, seventh and eighth, but with perhaps some additions and alterations by Guru Gobind Singh.

(b) The compositions of certain Bhagats (saints), mostly sectarian Hindus, and who are usually given as sixteen in number.

(c) The verses of certain Bhats (rhapsodists)—followers of Nanak and some of his successors.

The numbers and the names of the saints are not always the same in copies of the Adi Granth; and thus modern compilers or copyists have assumed to themselves the power of rejecting or sanctioning particular writings. To the sixteen Bhagats are usually added two Doms (chanters) who recited before Arjan, and who caught some of his spirit and Rababi (stringed instrument).

The Adi Granth was compiled by Guru Arjan (5th Guru), who dictated it to Bhai Gur Das (died 1629 AD). He was the first cousin of the mother of Guru Arjan. The Granth has subsequently received a few additions at the hand of Guru Arjan's successors.

Contents of the Adi Granth

1. Japji (Jap), called the Mul Mantra, is the special prayer of initiation of the Guru Nanak. It occupies about seven pages and consists of forty slokas, called Pauri, of irregular lengths. It means literally, the remembrance or admonisher, from Jap, to remember. It was written by Gruu Nanak and is to be repeated each morning. The mode of composition implies the presence of a questioner and an answer, and the Sikhs believe that the questioner to have been the disciple Angad.
2. Sodar Ras. The evening prayer of the Sikhs. It occupies about three and a half pages, and it was composed by Nanak, but has additions by Guru Ram Das and Guru

Arjan.

3. Kirti Sohaila. A prayer repeated before going to sleep. It occupies a page and a line. It was by Nanak, but has additions by Guru Ramdas and Arjan, and one verse it attributed to Guru Gobind Singh. Kirti is from Sanskrit Kirti, to praise, to celebrate, and Sohila a marriage song is a song of rejoicing.
4. The next portion of the Granth is divided into thirty-one sections, known by their distinguishing forms of verse, as follows:

Sri Rag, Maja, Gauri, Asa, Gujri, Dev Gandhari, Bihagra, Wad Hans, Sorath, Dhanasri, Jait Sri, Todi, Bairavi, Tailang, Sudhi, Bilwal, Gaund, Ram Kali, Nat Narayan, Mali Gaura, Maru, Tukhari, Kedara, Bhairon, Basant, Sarang, Malhar, Kanhra, Kalian, Prabhati, Jai Jaiwanti.

The Ragas occupie about 1339 pages and is by far the greater portion of the entire Granth. Each subdivision is the composition of one or more Gurus, or of one or more Bhagats or holy men, of a Guru with or without aid of a Bhagat (saint).

The hymns of the Gurus and Saints are not arranged in the Adi Granth according to their authors, but according to the thirty-one Ragas or musical measures to which they were composed.

The first nine Gurus adopted the name Nanak as their nom de plume, and their compositions are distinguished by Mohallas (wives of the Lord). The Gurus regarded themselves as wives of the Lord. Thus the compositions of Guru Nanak are styled Mohalla one; the composition of Guru Angad, the second Mohalla; the compositions of Guru Amar Das, the third Mohalla, and so on. After the hymns of the Gurus are found the hymns of the Bhagats (saints) under their several musical measures.

Guru Gobind Singh added 115 hymns of his father (Guru Tegh Bahadur) in the new recension prepared by him because the original copy of the Adi Granth was in the possession of Dhirmal (brother of the seventh Guru, Guru Har Rai), who was reluctant to part with it. The new copy of the Adi Granth was prepared at Damdama Sahib in 1706. Before his death, Guru Gobind Singh conferred Guruship on the scripture at Nander in 1708 and named it the Guru Granth Sahib.

Adi Granth or Guru Granth Sahib and its contributors

Sikh Gurus	No, of hymns (Place & date of death)
Guru Nanak	947 hymns (Nankana, 14609 AD)
Guru Angad Dev	63 Shlokas (Sarai Mata (Pb).
Guru Amar Das	863 hymns (Basarke (Pb). 1479 AD)
Guru Ram Das	638 hymns (Lahore. 1534 AD)
Guru Arjan Dev	2312 hymns (Gobindwal 1563 AD)
Guru Tegh Bahadur	115 hymns (Amritsar 1622 AD)

Pre Nanak Saints

Jaidev	2 hymns (Bengal 1170 AD)
Sheikh Farid	4 hymns (Pan jab 1173 AD)
Namdev	62 hymns (Maharashtra 1270 AD)
Trilochan	5 hymns (Maharashtra 1267 AD)
Parmanand	1 hymn (Maharashtra)
Sadhna	1 hymn (Sind)
Beri	3 hymns (Not known)
Ramananda	1 hymn (U.P.)
Dhanna	4 hymns (Rajasthan)
Pipa	1 hymn (Gagraungarh
Sain	1 hymn (Not known)
Kabir	534 hymns (Benaras 1398 AD)
Ravidas	41hymns (1430 AD)

Saints or poets who lived during the time of the Guru

Bhikan	(2 hymns)
Sur Das	(2 hymns)
Sundar	6 Pauri)
Shalokas	(3 hymns)

Kal	(46 Swayyas)
Kalsar	(4 Swayyas)
Tar	(1 Swayyas)
Jalap	(4 Swayyas)
Jal	(1 Swayyas)
Kirnt	(8 Swayyas)
Sal	(3 Swayyas)
Bhal	(1 Swayyas)
Nal	(6 Swayyas)
Bhikha	(2 Swayyas)
Jalan	(1 Swayyas)
Das	(7 Swayyas
Gayand	(5 Swayyas)
Sewak	(7 Swayyas)
Mathura	(10 Swayyas)
Bal	(5 Swayyas)
Harbans	(2 Swayyas)
Dalwant and Satta	(1Var of 8 Pauris)

Bhog

In Sanskrit the Bhog means to enjoy or partake something, but is commonly used to denote the conclusion of any sacred writing of Nanak and Arjan, of Kabir, Shah Farid, and other reformers. It contains the composition of nine Bhatta (rhapsodists) who attached themselves to Guru Amardas, Guru Ram Das and Guru Arjan.

The Bhog commences with 4 Sloks (couplets) in Sanskrit by Nanak, which are followed by 67 Sanskrit Sloks in one metre by Guru Arjan, and then by 24 in another metre by the same Guru. There are also 23 Sloks in Panjabi by Guru Arjan which contain praises of Amritsar. These are followed by 243 Sloks of Kabir, and 130 by Shah Farid, and others, containing some saying of Guru Arjan, and so on to the end.

The nine Bhats who contributed 123 Sabad etc. to the Bhog are named as follows:

1. Bhikha (follower of Guru Amardas)

2. Kal (follower of Gur Ramdas)
3. Kal Shar
4. Jalap (follower of Guru Arjan)
5. Nal
6. Mathura
7. Bhal
8. Kirat

These names are evidently fanciful, and perhaps fictitious; in the book called the Guru Bilas, only eight Bhats are enumerated, and all the names, except Bal, are different from those in the Granth.

Supplement to the Granth

Bhog ki Bani, or epilogue of the conclusion. It contains about seven pages and contains hymns of the first Guru, Nanak's admonition to the Malhar Raga; the Ratan Mala of the Nanak, Hakikat or circumstances of Sivnab, Raja of Ceylon. It is assumed that this composition is by Bhai Bhanu, a devotee of Guru Gobind Singh.

It is generally agreed that there were the following recensions of the Adi Granth:

1. The first compiled by Guru Arjan and installed in AD 1504.
2. The second recension is called Bhai Bano Ki Bir had two additional hymns—one by Surdas and the other by Mira Bai and several poems.

The tenth and the last Guru Gobind instructed his followers that after him, the holy Granth, as the voice of the Gurus and saints, was to be respected as the Guru himself. The holy book is wrapped in a fine cloth, in any room which is reserved for praying only.

Adi Granth—arrangement of its hymns

Guru Arjan Dev compiled Adi Granth/Guru Granth Sahib. In Sikhism worship consisted of singing the hymns from the Adi Granth and performing the rituals concerned with that. The Gurus laid down which hymns to be sung and the right ritual to be performed by the followers. Guru Nanak had preserved his own compositions and also of some saints. At the time of his death he passed them on to his successor Guru Angad. Similarly Guru Angad and Amar Das preserved their own hymns. This collection was called Bani Pothi or Book of hymns. The hymns of Bani Pothi were arranged by Guru Amar Das's grandson, Sahansar Ram, son of Mohan, in two volumes of 300 and 224 leaves. The hymns contained some hymns of Jaidev, Kabir, Ravidas, Sain and Trilochan. These volumes were in the possession of Mohan, son of Guru Amar Das. Mohan gave these two manuscripts to Guru Arjan after a lot of persuasion by the Guru.

On his return the Guru visited Khadur and there he met Guru Angad's eldest son Datu who also gave him some material belonging to the Gurus. This contained Sri Rag of Guru Nanak and some other hymns which were not included in Bani Pothi. He reached Amritsar and with the help of Bhai Gurdas, a scholar of Sanskrit, Persian, Hindi and Panjabi, he put them in the right order. Bhai Gurdas wrote the Adi Granth on loose sheets. He was a nephew of Guru Amar Das and the first cousin of the mother of Guru Arjan. A copy of the holy Granth Sahib written by him exists at Kartarpur near Jallandhar.

It was arranged in three parts. The first part consists of morning and evening prayers, Guru Nanak's Japji and other devotional hymns. It begins with the confession of faith, or credo, and ends with the prayers offered before retiring to rest at night.

The second part is the main body containing thirty-one Ragas. The peculiarity of Ragas is that it is based on the theory that each musical sound corresponds to some emotions of the human heart. When any particular sound predominates in a tune, that tune is supposed to give rise to a peculiar Rag, or emotion; hence it follows that there being generally reckoned six primary Ragas, each of which has five or six assistant Raginis, and eight subordinate Ragas. This would give a total of 84 Ragas and Raginis. The Hindu classical music was only music known to the compilers of the Holy book, and each Raga is specially applicable to some season of the year, or some time of the day. With the minuteness of details, which characterises the Hindu science, the day is divided into numerous portions, providing accommodation for Ragas applicable to midnight, early morning, sunrise, etc., down to evening and night again. The Hindus have divided the full day into 8 Pahars each of which contains 8 gharis giving a total of 64 gharis for the entire day. If we allow 2 gharis for every Raga, we get 32 Ragas; the doubt as to the number arising from the fact that, after the book had been arranged by the Fifth Guru Arjan, the Ninth Guru Tegh Bahadur, composed four hymns in a peculiar strain, which have been classed as separate Raga and inserted, sometimes in the middle of the book, and sometimes at the end. The first three Ragas (Sri Rag, Majh and Gauri) represent morning, mid-day and evening. Towards the end of the Granth a similar indication of method is observable; for the Ragas Bhairau, Basant, Sarang, and Malar follow each other in succession and these Ragas represent Autumn, Spring, Summer, and the Rains. The hymns which are to be sung in a particular Raga were first placed together; and were then arranged under the following heads:

1. Chaupadas, containing an average of four verses each.
2. Ashtapadis, containing an average of eight verses each.
3. Special long poems.
4. Chhants, consisting of 6-line verses.
5. Special short poems.
6. Vars, consisting of two or more Shloks, and a Pauri, or concluding stanza.
7. Poems of the Bhagats, or Saints.

The hymns are further classified, under these seven heads,

according to their authorship. The hymns are being placed first in chronological order of the Gurus, followed by those of the saints, according to a well-defined order of precedence, in which all the Hindu writers come before the Muhammadan saint Sheikh Farid. He is followed by Mira Bai, a female devotee of Lord Krishna. Mira Bai seems to have been excluded from the holy book.

The third part is called Bhog ki Bani. The arrangement of this is in accordance with that of the Rig Veda; the first Mandala of which is liturgical, followed by various sets of hymns, and ending with the long and short hymns, or miscellaneous collections. It includes panegyrics of the first five Gurus, some additional hymns of Guru Nanak, Amar Das, Ram Das, Arjan Dev and Tegh Bahadur, and Swayyas of Guru Arjan Dev and sayings of Farid and Kabir, and of eleven bards. It concludes with Mundavani, in which Guru Arjan explains the purpose of the sacred book. The arrangement of the pages in the holy book is as follows:-

Japji 1-7; Musical hymns 8-1351, Sanskrit Shalokas 1352-59, Gatha 1359-61, Funhe 1361-62, Chaubole 1363-64, Shalokas of Kabir and Farid 1364-84, Swayyas of the Gurus and Bhatts 1384-1408, Shalokas of the Gurus 1409-28, Ragmala or Index of musical measures 1429-30.

The hymns were not given in chronological order according to the Gurus but they were adjusted in accordance with thirty-one Ragas or musical measures such as Asa, Sorath and Ramkali. There are 14 Ragas and 17 Raginis. The holy book is arranged on a fourfold basis: (1) Ragas or tunes in which the hymns were to be recited, (2) metre of the hymns, (3) authorship, and (4) key, clef or ghar. Guru Arjan used 31 Ragas only out of 84. Under each particular Raga the hymns of Guru Nanak are given first are called Mahalla Pahila or One, Mahalla Two for Guru Angad, Mahalla Three for Guru Amar Das, Mahalla Four for Guru Ram Das, and Mahalla Five for Guru Arjan. The Adi Granth contains only prayers and devotional songs and not a word about the lives of the Gurus. In his last hymn Guru Arjan placed three things – Truth,

Harmony and Wisdom. These are seasoned with the Name of God, which is the basis of all. Whoever eats and enjoys it, shall be saved.

Guru Arjan named it Pothi Sahib. Pothi Parmeshwar ka than (the book is the abode of God). The book was completed in Savan Samvat 1661 (July 1604), and the Guru gave it to Bhai Bano to get it bound at Lahore. Bhai Bano got it copied and two bound volumes were presented to the Guru. The Guru put his signature on the second volume to certify its authenticity. The original volume was installed in Hari Mandar (Golden temple) at Amritsar on 16 August 1604.

Dasam Granth (book of the tenth Guru, Guru Gobind Singh, 1666-1708)

The Guru's manuscript of Dasam Granth was drowned in the river Sarsa on 22 December 1704. A few copies of many of his works were made by some of his fifty-two poets and scholars in his Durbar (court). Later the compilation of the Dasam Granth was undertaken by Bhai Mani Singh at the request of Mata Sundri, the widow of Guru Gobind Singh. Four copies of the Dasam Granth were made, and the copies were kept at Akal Takht (Amritsar), Patna, Anandpur and Damdama Sahib.

Like the Adi Granth, the book of Guru Gobind is metrical throughout, but the versification frequently varies. It is written in the Hindi dialect, and in Gurmukhi script, except the concluding portion, the language of which is Persian, while the alphabet continue in Gurmukhi. The Hindi of Guru Gobind is almost such as is spoken in the Gangetic provinces, and has few peculiarities of the Panjabi dialect.

Guru Gobind was a saint-soldier and he also combined the rare qualities of a great soldier and a great writer. Most of his writing is imbued with the spirit of the sword. His martial poetry is a more direct and powerful influence upon the opinions and feelings of the people. As in Bhagvad Gita Lord Krishna teaches Arjuna the duties of warrior, similarly the

Guru teaches his followers to carry on fighting until we achieve victory for the protection of Dharma, for the destruction of the evil rule of Mughals and to establish righteousness.

All the works of the Guru contain a hero who is a brave warrior full of courage, high-minded, generous, upright and just. In Krishna Avtar the Guru explains that the purpose of writing this is to inspire his followers for a holy war (dharma yudh). He wishes to remove any feeling of inferiority in fighting the Muslim rulers. The Guru gave example of Goddess Durga, being a woman, who killed the demons and why his Khalsa (pure army) would remain behind and not follow the examples of the Goddess. His message contains hope, courage, devotion, freedom and self-reliance.

It is known that Guru Gobind Singh employed in his court the poets and musicians dismissed by Aurganzeb, when he left for the Deccan in 1682. The Guru started writing in 1684 at Anandur at the age of eighteen. In Krishna Avtar he says that he had composed about a thousand verses at Anandpur before he left for Paonta. The Guru wrote a good deal of his poetry at Paonta from 1685 to 1688.

One character of the Dasam Granth is considered to be narrative and historical, namely, the Bachitr Natak, the Persian Hikayats, or stories, also partakes of that character, from the circumstances attending their composition and the nature of some allusion made in them. The other portions of this Granth are more mythological than the first book, and it also partakes more of a worldly character throughout, although it contains many noble allusions to the unity of Godhead, and to the greatness and goodness of the Ruler of the Universe.

Five chapters, or portions only, and the commencement of the sixth, are attributed to Guru Gobind himself; the remainder, by far the larger portion, is said to have been composed by four scribes in the service of the Guru; partly, perhaps, agreeably to his dictation. The names of Sham and Ram occurs as two of the writers, but, in truth, little is known of the authorship of the portions in question.

The holy book of the Guru contains divine prayers, tales of

heroism and morality from ancient Indian literature of old sages, saints and seers. It also consists of historical, religious, philosophical and secular literature. The works of the Guru are in Awadhi, Braj Bhasha, Hindi, Panjabi and Persian with some Arabic words. They are in Gurmukhi script. Zafar Namas, Hikayat and Fatah Nama are in Persian script. Some hymns are in Majha Panjabi. They are all in poetry in different metres.

The Dasam Granth reveals the national spirit throughout by telling us heroic stories of the great deeds of our ancestors. The characters from the Puranic literature have been converted into great warriors using swords with great control against demons. The battles show bravery and triumph of Gods and Goddesses. In these battles woman and children have been shown fighting along with men. Every one took part in the struggle for virtue against vice, for goodness against evil, and for truth against falsehood. Freedom fighters are highly praised for opposing tyranny and oppression. The stories appeal to all and arose a feeling of nationalism and patriotism. By his writings and sermons to his followers, he was preparing them for the forthcoming fight against the Muslim rulers.

In Ram Avtar the Guru gave some idea of heavenly life, as the Guru believed that Dharam Yudh (righteous war) and worship to God would take us to heaven. For that reason he did not consider the different between war and heaven.

The Dasam Granth formed a quarto volume of 1066 pages, each page consisting of 23 lines, each line of 38 to 41 letters. It consist of:

(1) Akal Ustat—272 verses,
(2) Bachitra Natak—471 verses,
(3) Chandi Charitra, First version—233 verses and Second version—262 verses,
(4) Chandi di Var—55 verses,
(5) Chaubir Avtar—1201 verses,
(6) Fatah Nama—24 verses,
(7) Gian Prabodh—336 verses,
(8) Hikayat—756 verses,

(9) Jap—199 verses,
(10) Mir Mahndi—10 verses,
(11) Pakhian Charitra—7569 verses,
(12) Ram Avtar and Krishna Avtar—4370 verses
(13) Shabad Patshai Das—10 verses
(14) Shastar Nam Mala—1323 verses
(15) Swayyas—33 verses
(16) Zafar Nama—111 verses
(17) Miscellaneous—59 verses

The Akal Ustat

It is in praise of the Almighty who is called Akal Purkh, who is timeless, formless and all-pervading, who is also both the creator and destroyer. There is no salvation without his worship. A hymn commonly read in the morning. It occupies 23 pages. Its language is a mixture of Sanskrit, Braj Bhasha, Persian and Arabic. It is a collection of many subjects which were composed at different times and then compiled together

Bachitra Natak (wondrous tale)

The Bachitra Natak occupies 24 pages of the Granth and it describes:

(a) Mythological history of the Gurus. It is an autobiography written at Anandpur in 1692 when he was 26 years old. He describes the Bedi Vansh (Bedi dynasty) of Guru Nanak and Sodhi Vansh (Sodhi dynasty) of his family. He discusses the nine Gurus and sacrifice of his father (Guru Tegh Bahadur). He tells his own penance in an earlier life at the snowy mountains of Hemkunth, his present birth and his mission.

(b) An account of his mission or reformation, He gives his own battles in which he was commander-in-chief of his army. Gives his description of warfare with Himalayan chiefs and the imperial forces.

(c) It is divided into fourteen sections; but the first is devoted to the praises of the Almighty, and the last is of similar tenor, with an addition to the effect that he would hereafter relate his visions of the past and his experiences of the present world.

Chandi Charitra (wonders of Chandi Goddess)

There are two portions called Chandi Charitra, Ukt Bilas and Chandi Charitra Dwityas. It relates to the destruction of eight Titans or Dwityas by Chandi Goddess. It occupies 20 pages. They are based on Markandeya Purana, and are in Hindi.

The names of Dwityas destroyed are as follows:

(1) Madhu Kitab, (2) Mah Khasur, (3) Dhima Lochan, (4) Chan, (5) Mund, (6) Rakaj Bij, (7) Nishumb and (8) Shumb.

The second portion of 262 verses, contains the same legend as the greater Chandi narrated in a different metre. It occupies about 14 pages.

Chandi di Var or Var Sri Bhagauti (Chandi) Ji di

A supplement to the legends of Chandi. It occupies about six pages. It is based on the Puranas and it is in Panjabi. The first 25 verses form the invocation to the holy sword. The next six verses give background, and the rest of the poem describes the exciting battle scenes. The Goddess Durga fought a holy war against demons. She rode on a roaring tiger, brandishing sword, to terrify her enemies and demons. Piercing arrows fell like rain. Wave after wave of warriors came forward, delivered the assault and fell to the ground by the sword of the Goddess

In the battlefield Goddess Durga is always victorious. She is the friend of the weak. She is the symbol of courage, superior moral force and spiritual strength. It was fight between good and evil, and between virtues and vice depicted by the Guru.

Chaubis Avtar (24 incarnations)

These verses occupy about 348 pages in Hindi. In this work 24 incarnations of Brahma,Vishnu, Rama, Krishna and Arjan are described in 1201 verses. These incarnations fought against evil-doers to protect the good and virtuous people. At the end a note states that the work was completed in 1755 Vikram (1698 AD) in the month of Har (June-July) on the banks of river Satluj near the foot of Naina Devi Hill. The names of the incarnations are as follows:

(1) The Fish or Machh, (2) Tortoise or Kurma, (3) The Lion or Nara, (4) Narayan, (5) Mohini, (6) The boar, Varah, (7) The man-lion or Narasimha, (8) The Dwarf or Barwan, (9) Paras Ram, (10) Brahma, (11) Rudra, (12) Jalandar, (13) Vishnu, (14) No name specified, (15) Arhant Dev (considered to be the founder of the sect of Saraugis of the Jain persuasion, or indeed the great Jain prophet himself, (16) Man Raja, (17) The Sun or Suraj, (18) Dhanantar—the doctor or physician, (19) The moon or Chandrama, (20) Ram, (21) Krishna, (22) Nar – meaning Arjan, (23) Bodh, (24) Kalki – to appear at the end of the Kalyug or when the sins of men are at their height.

Fatah Namah

It is a short letter containing 24 couplets in Persian addressed to Aurangzeb from Jaipura near Jagraon.

Gian Prabodh

It contains 336 verses in praise of God, who is formless, colourless, casteless and creedless:
Atma Ram asks Parmatma who is the most marvellous hero with unlimited power and grandeur. Parmatma replies it is Brahma, who is unconditioned, strongest, yet most merciful.

Hikayats (tales)

These comprise twelve stories in 866 Slokas of two lines each. They are written in the Persian language and Gurmukhi character, and they were composed by the Guru as an admonitory of Aurangzeb, and were sent to the Emperor through Daya Singh and four other Sikhs. A letter written in a pointed manner, which, however, does not form a portion of the Granth, accompanied the tales.

Jap

It is the supplement or complement of the Japji of Guru Nanak, a prayer to be read or repeated in the morning, as it continues to be by pious Sikhs. Jap is a morning prayer of the Khalsa and Japji of Guru Nanak is a morning prayer for all the Sikhs (Sahajdaris and Khalsa). It comprises 198 distchs (verses), and occupies about seven pages, the termination of a verse and the end of a line not being the same. The Guru gives about 950 names of God in the Jap. It was perhaps the first composition written about 1684.

God is the Supreme Power. He is most beautiful, bountiful, unborn, changeless and merciful, wielder of arms and present everywhere. The language is Hindi and Sanskrit and also includes a few Arabic words.

Krishna Avtar

It was composed in 1688 before the battle of Bhangani. It contains heroic and parental sentiments. In verse 10 the Guru says that why should He whose form and colour are not known be called black? You will escape from the net of Death when you cling to His feet.

Mir Mahndi

It deals with the incarnation of Mir Mahndi or Midhi Mir. It is a supplement to the twenty-four incarnations, Mahndi, it is said, will appear when the mission of Kalki is fulfilled. It occupies less than a page.

No name entered but known as the Avtars of Brahma. An account of the seven incarnations of Brahma, followed by some account of eight Rajas of bygone times. It occupies about 18 pages. The names of incarnations are as follows:

(1) Valmik, (2) Kashap, (3) Shukar, (4) Batchess, (5)

Vyasi, (6) Khasht Rikhi – Rishi of six sages, (7) Kaul Das.

No name entered but known as the Avtars of Rudr or Lord Shiva. It comprises 56 pages; and two incarnations only are mentioned, namely Dat and Parasnath.

Pakhian Charitra or Istri Charitra or tales of women
There are 404 stories, illustrative of the character and disposition of women. A stepmother became enamoured of her stepson, the heir to a monarchy, who, however, would not gratify her desires, whereupon she represented to her husband that his first-born had made attempts upon her honour. The Raja ordered the son to be put to death, but his Ministers interfered, and procured a respite. They then enlarged in a series of stories upon the nature of women, and at length the Raja became sensible to the guilt of his wife's mind, and of his own rashness. These stories occupy 446 pages or nearly half of the Granth. The name of Sham also occurs as the writer of one or more of them.

There was a reason for these stories. He wanted to warn his followers of the wiles of women. The Guru knew that man's weakness at young age is woman. Many young men were recruiting themselves in Guru's army. At a young age the sex power is at its height. The Guru wanted to check their tendency towards women. 78 stories are devoted to the intelligence, bravery and devotion of women, 269 stories depict wiles and ruses of women, 28 stories discuss man's deceit and cunning in relation to women, 10 stories deal with the folly of drinking, opium eating and gambling and many describe folk tales.

Ram Avtar

It was written in 1698 on the banks of the Satluj. In Ram Avtar he offered his warriors of Dharam Yudh (righteous war) celestial maidens. As the mighty warriors slashed and struck at the enemy, each heavenly maiden was encouraging every individual hero. As long as you lay down your life in Dharam Yudh (righteous war), you will be in my arms, and I will take you to heaven.

Shabad Padshahi Da or Hazar Shabd

These ten verses only in most Granths, occupying about two pages. Hazar (thousand) is not understood in its literal sense of a thousand, but as implying invaluable or excellent. They are laudatory of the Creator and not creation, and deprecate the adoration of saints and divinities. These ten verses insist on the worship of one God only.

The idea of one God was first mentioned in Rig Veda. It was beautifully brought out in one of the mantras of the Rig Veda, which declares that reality is one and that sages call it by different names – Indra, Varuna, Agni etc. The Sanskrit verses of the Rig Veda are as follows:

Indram mitram varunam agnim ahuh
Atho divyas sa suparno garutman
Ekam sad vipra bahudha vadanti
Aanim yamam matarisvanam ahuh

Shastra Nam Mala

The string of weapons. The names of the various weapons are recapitulated, the weapons are praised, and Gobind terms them collectively his Guru or guide. Amongst the weapons the most important position is assigned to sword.

Swayyas/ Sri Mukh Vak Swayyas

The Guru dwells on the worship of formless God. The verses are recited during the preparation of Amrit to be administered at baptism. The Guru as a sermon on divinity composed—Sri Mukh Vak Swayyas of voice of the Guru in 32 verses. They are complementary to the Vedas and Puran. They occupy about three-and-a-half pages.

Zafar Nama

The Zafar Nama is in Persian poetry containing 111 verses. It was written in February 1705. It was written when the Guru was hiding in exile, his army was destroyed by the Mughals, his two elder sons were killed in the battle of Chamkaur, his wives were not with him and his two younger sons were bricked alive at Sarhind. In the Zafar Nama the Guru scolds Aurangzeb for his faithlessness, treachery, hypocrisy veiled under religious garb. He particularly criticises Aurangzeb for violating solemn promises and religious oaths. The Guru pleaded for open diplomacy, and the practice of moral values in political matters. He calls the Emperor oath-breaker and warns him of the consequence of his tyrannous acts.

Adi Granth (Guru Granth Sahib) and the Dasam Granth—comparison.

Similarity

Both believe in one Supreme Being, a personal God, merciful and kind.

Both believe that God is all pervading, unborn, formless and timeless.

Both lay emphasis on meditation i.e. repetition of the Name of God to achieve salvation.

Both believe in the law of Karma and transmigration of the soul.

Both have faith in Sach Khand.

Both emphasise on the devotion to the Guru, who is a perfect man but not God.

Both believe in casteless and classless society, and equality between men and women.

Both are in poetry form and in Gurmukhi script.

Difference

The main difference between the two is that of object. The Adi Granth aims at gaining peace of mind and complete surrender to God. The Dasam Granth believes in a holy war (Dharam Yudh) against tyranny and fanaticism.

God of the Adi Granth is the God of Truth. God of the Dasam

Granth is the God of justice, ready to strike at the tyrant, autocrat and the despot.

The Adi Granth is full of devotion, meditation, grace of the Guru and God. The Dasam Granth depicts scenes of battles, arms, and weapons, intrigues of women.

Festivals, dances, games, pilgrimages in Sikhism

Festivals

The Sikh festivals are generally called Gurpurbs connected with the death anniversaries of the Gurus or special historical events like Baisakhi, Holla Mohalla, etc. Festivals are observed in all Gurdwaras with worship, special prayers, hymn-singing, recitation of poems, and also Langar (free kitchen food). The main festivals are as under:

1. *Guru Nanak's birthday.* Though the actual birthday is on 15 April 1469, but it is tradionally celebrated on Puranmashi day in Katak (October/November). The date varies according to lunar calendar.
2. *Guru Gobind Singh's birthday.* The actual birthday is on 22 December 1666. It is celebrated according to the Bikrami calendar (December/January). The main celebration is in Patna (Gurdwara Janamasathan) where he was born.
3. *Baisakhi.* Apart from being a harvest festival in the Panjab, it was on this day that Guru Gobind Singh established the Khalsa brotherhood, actually on 30 March 1699. However it is celebrated on 13 April every year.
4. *Diwali.* This festival falls in October/November is celebrated because it was on this day in 1621 that Guru Hargobind reached Amritsar after his release from Gwalior prison. The Golden Temple is especially decorated for this event. Illuminations, fireworks and display of treasures, relics and weapons are also held there.
5. *Holla Mohalla.* In place of Holi, Guru Gobind Singh started the celebration of Holla Mohalla when mock battles, military exercises, contests in swordsmanship,

archery, wrestling, fencing are held. It is held at Fatehgarh Sahib in Panjab.

6. There are certain Gurparbs celebrated to commemorate certain important events, for example, Guru Arjan's martyrdom. It generally falls in June and is celebrated in all the Gurdwaras. Guru Teghbahadur's martyrdom, a special celebration is held at Gurdwara Sisganj and Gurdwara Rikabganj in Delhi. It generally falls in November. Foundation of the city of Amritsar by Guru Ramdas, a special function is at the Golden Temple (Amritsar).
7. Two celebrations are held every year to commemorate (a) the installation of the Adi Granth/Guru Granth Sahib in the Golden Temple in August 1604, and (b) the installation of Guru Granth Sahib as the permanent Guru by Guru Gobind Singh (at Nander in October 1708). It is called Guru Granth Guryal Gurparb.

The items of the celebration may include the following, depending on resources:

a. Processions with brass bands, horses, singers, led by the Panj Payaras.
b. Akhand Path starts two days before the day of celebration with the Bhog on the day of celebration.
c. Whole day programme beginning with Asa-di-var, kirtan, katha, lectures, langar, kirtan darbar/kavi darbar.
d. Public functions in public halls with seminars, lectures and discussions.
e. Competitions in Kirtan/Panjabi elocution/Gurbani recitation, games and sports, fireworks, exhibition of Sikh literature.

Kartik Purnamashi

Spring and autumn are the two harvest festive seasons in India, which are very popular with the people. Kartik Purnamashi (October-November) brings up the rear of this glittering array of festivals, e.g. Diwali, Dussehra etc.

In Sikhism Kartik Purnamashi is very important for the following reasons:

Bhai Bala's Janam Sakhi is earliest record, which says that Nanak was born on Kartik Purnamashi. Trilochan Singh, the biographer of Guru Nanak upholds Kartik Purnamashi as the date of Nanak's birth.

During Guru Nanak's time it was considered a religious act of merit to bathe in a nearby river. Nanak used to bathe in a rivulet called Kali Bein, which flowed near, by this town of Sultanpur. According to Mohsin Fani, Nanak used to sing hymns in praise of God in the presence of people gathered on the bank of this river. Simultaneously he began purifying his body and soul by reducing his food and living on cow-milk and butter. Finally he lived on water and air only. Nanak became very weak and one day after his bath he went to take rest in a cave in the bank of river Bein and there he went into a trance. It was at dawn on the full-moon-day in Kartik, 1496, that Nanak regained consciousness, and with it came enlightenment like that of the great Buddha. On Kartik Purnamashi day Nanak got the divine light and that is why it is very important to the Sikhs and Hindus and other devotees of Guru Nanak.

Dances

Bhangra

This is the most popular and best-known dance of the Panjab, performed on all festive occasions. Forming a large circle the dancers start going round, so that during the performance as many dancers as possible can join in the circle from time to time even if the have not joined in the start. The drummer takes his place in the centre of the circle, and as he plays his rhythmic beats, every now and then he gives his signal to the dancers to increase their speed. The two or three dancers who stand just behind the drummer lead the movements. There are lively movements of whirling round and round, beating of feet, clapping of their sticks, and as they get into the spirit of the dance, they cry Hoi-Hoi (up, up) to raise the excitement and fun of the dance, as they leap into the air. Then at intervals, there is a short pause in the dancing, and a boli (traditional folk song of the Panjab) is recited in the rhythm. Following this, the dance start once again. This dance has its usual season, which commences with the sowing of the wheat and concludes with the Baisakhi festival. The dance is done by men by the accompaniment of song and the dholak. The men are usually dressed in bright coloured clothes and turbans. This is the most popular dance of all Panjabis.

Giddha/Gidda

Panjabi women dance and sing. It is called Giddha. Just as the Bhangara is entirely done by men, so the Gidda is done exclusively by the women of Panjab at festival time and during the sowing and harvesting of the wheat crop. With a long tradition behind it, this dance is noteworthy for its graceful movements, and the lively simple melody that accompanies it. Forming a circle, the women go round and round, waving their arms and supple wrists, raising the arms and turning and moving forward and backward. Dressed in bright coloured Salwar-Kamij (wide trouser and tunic) with contrasting scarves, they make a pretty picture in the old pastoral dance of the region.

Games

Chaupat – a game of dice for men.

*Chichi-*Chich Ganderian. A game for boys and girls between the age of five and twelve years. It involves of drawing of vertical lines as many times as possible by two opposing parties of boys and girls. Some hides and others go to mark lines on the wall; when the latter return the former go to erase those lines, and when they come back, all the children go to see whether all lines have been erased or not. They count those lines, which have not been erased, and the party who marked the lines is entitled to get something from the other party.

Gulli Danda. It is a very common game between the boys. It is an Indian version of cricket. The game is also called tip-cat (a cat is a pointed piece of wood). It is a game in which the cat is struck with a cat-stick and made to spring up and then it is hit with the stick.

Gutka-Bazi. Fencing with sticks and swords.

Kabbadi. A very popular game among the boys and girls in Panjab and now it is also, popular in other parts of India. There are two sides. A player from one side approaches the other. He has to touch one of the opponents and return in one breath calling out 'Kabbadi-Kabbadi' all the while. The other side does its best to take him/her prisoner. If he/she succeeds, the opponent touched is out, otherwise he/she falls out. There are two varieties of game bari kabbadi and lammi kabbadi.

Kikkli. Game played by young girls by holding hands, stretching backwards and going round and round.

Kite flying (Patang Bazi). It is very common in northern India.

Lattu. A game for children – a wooden ball is suspended from a string.

Lukan-mitti. Hide and seek is a very popular game among children.

Shatranj. A game of chess.

Sohli. Gambling with shells (kauris).

Wrestling. It is a very popular game among men.

Pilgrimages – Gurdwaras

In Gurbani it is mentioned that devotion to God and the Guru is the true pilgrimage. The term 'the sixty-eight places of pilgrimages' is used frequently in the Holy Granth, and it says that for the achievement of oneness with God, the remembrance of the name of God and thoughts about the attributes of God and the singing of His praises are far better than pilgrimage to sixty-eight places as mentioned in Hinduism. Anyway most of the Sikhs visit the following Gurdwaras and regard them as being very meritorious for good luck, and prosperity for themselves and their families. All the following Gurdwaras are mentioned alphabetically.

Akal Takht, Amritsar (eternal throne or seat of temporal authority) is one of the five Sikh shrines of great importance to the Sikhs. The Akal Takht is concerned with Guru Hargobind and the other four are connected with Fguru Gobind Singh.

Anand Garh, Kila (fort) Gurdwara. It is situated about 3 to 4 kms. of the south of Anandpur city. Inside this fort is a big baoli (deep well). The steps leading to it are more than 200 in number. A beautiful garden is located near the baoli.

Bandhi Chhor Sahib. Gurdwara built at Gwalior to commemorate the release of Guru Hargobind. By the orders of the Emperor Jahangir.

Bangla Sahib, New Delhi. This Gurdwara is dedicated to the memory of Guru Harkrishan (8th Guru), who stayed there at the residence of Raja Jai Singh of Jaipur. The dome of the Guedwara has been covered with gold-plate with voluntary donations of the congregation. A secondary school for girls and a clinic have been established by the management board. The free kitchen serves food to the visitors to the shrine.

Baoli Sahib

Guru Amar Das (1479-1574) was nominated as Guru in 1552 at the age of 73. He was born in a Bhalla Khatri family at a village Basarke about 13 kilometres from Amritsar. The old Guru did a lot of social work and decided to give the Sikhs a sacred well (Baoli) at Goindwal, near Amritsar, which would be different from other wells prevalent at that time. The digging of the Baoli started in 1556 and completed in 1559. He did not want the devotees to draw water with the use of rope and wanted them to reach the water by going down the steps. The well had 84 steps and the Guru told his devotees that whoever would repeat the Japji on every step, would escape from the wanderings in the wombs of the eight-four lakhs of living creatures. This ceaseless journey of soul of birth and death and rebirth is known as transmigration of soul in

Hinduism and Buddhism, signifying the flow of the soul from form to form, from body to body, or the re-embodiment of the soul in varying forms. The well, with its eighty-four steps corresponds to the eighty-four lakhs of existence in the transmigratory cycle of the Hindus. The Baoli (well) at Goindwal became a place of pilgrimage for the devotees (Sikhs and Hindus). Goindwal became a very famous place of pilgrimage during the time of the Guru.

Chaubara Sahib

It is a two-storied -building in Goindwal (near Amritsar) with an enclosed courtyard; it served as the residence of Guru Amar Das. The room used by him has its walls and ceiling artistically done up with glass and coloured stones set in multicoloured plasterwork. At this place the Guru was ceremoniously installed as the fourth Guru, and the fifth Guru (Arjan Dev) was also born there. Guru Amar Das and Guru Ram Das both died in this house at the ages of 95 and 47 respectively. On the first floor is a room which used to be occupied by Baba Mohan, son of t5he third Guru. He had with him the composition of the first three Gurus, and Guru Arjan obtained these compilations from him for compiling the Granth Sahib.

Damdama Sahib

It means a breathing place or halfway spot where the Sikh Gurus took some rest on their journeys. A number of Gurdwaras sanctified by the stay of Gurus are called Damdama Sahib. A few important ones are mentioned below:

The Gurdwara at Talwandi Sabo (17 miles from Bhatinda) is called Damdama Sahib because Guru Gobind Singh stayed here for nine months. He trained missionaries, and also had a revised edition of the Adi Granth/Guru Granth Sahib prepared by Bhai Mani Singh. A Historic Gurdwara at Delhi is also called Damdama Sahib (near New Delhi Nizamuddin Railway Station), where Guru Gobind Singh met the Emperor Bahadur Shah and discussed matters of mutual interest.

Damdama Sahib Gurdwara at Anandpur is connected with the memory of Guru Hargobind. Damdama Sahib Gurdwara is also situated between Khadar Sahib and Goindwal, where Guru Amar Das used to rest for some time, while carrying a pitcher of water for the bath of Guru Angad. In the years 1543-1552. Guru Tegh Bahadur during his travels in 1669, stayed at Dhubri (the capital of Kamrup) and visited the places where Guru Nanak preached the local people. Later a Gurdwara was built there called Damdama Sahib.

Dera Sahib (Lahore in Pakistan)

This is a Gurdwara built on the spot where Guru Arjan Dev was martyred in 1606. After going through various tortures, his body was thrown into the river Ravi. Maharaja Ranjit Singh renovated the building and also decorated it. A huge celebration takes place every year in June at this Gurdwara when devotees from India and abroad assemble to pay their homage to the Guru.

Dehra Baba Nanak Mandir/Gurdwara (in Gurdaspur district)

It is visited by Sikhs and Hindus on the occasion of Baisakhi, Puranmashi (October-November). Diwali and when Chola Sahib ceremony is observed (February-March). It was built in 1744 Samvat, and it contains the Samadhi of Guru Nanak. An Udasi Mahant who is celibate manages its affairs and the succession is governed by spiritual descent. A bhog offering of KarahParsad is offered morning. The present Gurdwara was built by Maharaja Ranjit Singh. An estate is also attached for its maintenance. There is an heirloom preserved near this spot, which is called Chola Sahib. It is the gown worn by Guru Nanak on his visit to Mecca. Originally the village was known as Kartarpur, and is the place where Guru Nanak passed away.

Golden Temple/ Hari Mandar or Harmandir Sahib (Darbar Sahib)

Hari means God and Mandir means temple (temple of God). It is situated in Amritsar and holds the foremost position among the Sikh shrines. It is the most important place of pilgrimage for the Singhs and the Sikhs and many Hindus. At the present place Guru Ram Das started the excavation work in 1577, but did not live to see it completed. His son and successor Guru Arjan Dev (5th Guru) got the tank (pool of nectar) completed in 1859, and Mian Mir (Muslim saint) laid the foundation stone of the temple at the request of Guru Arjan. The temple was completed in 1601 and the Granth Sahib was installed in 1604. People started living around the holy place, and it became known as Amritsar.

Many of the doors and domes of the temple are covered with gold plated copper sheets during the times of Maharaja Ranjit Singh, and therefore it is called Golden Temple. Very costly marble was used for the construction of the temple and the paving of steps, the path around the tank and the causeway. The inner walls of the temple are adorned with precious stones, frescoes and other artistic work. The temple has four doors, one in each direction. As one enters the shrine from the door facing the causeway, Sri Guru Granth Sahib is in front and some area around is cordoned by a low railing. There is enough space for musicians and the congregation. The door opposite leads to Har-Ki-Pauri where the pilgrims take the palmful of the sacred water (Amrit) from the tank. The first floor has a balcony overlooking the ground floor on all sides so that one can sit there, watch the proceedings below and listen to the Kirtan. Guru Arjan Dev used to sit there for meditation. Akhand Path (non-stop reading of the Granth Sahib) goes on there.

At the outer end of the pathway around the tank are bungas (rooms/houses) built by particular villages for their inhabitants to stay in during visits to the shrine. Next to that is Guru-ka-langar (community kitchen) where visitors have their meals free of charge every day. There is a thought provoking museum of Sikh history connected to the temple. Finally the architecture of the Golden Temple is worth appreciating and is a distinct quality of its own in temple architecture. (For more information SEE:—R.C. Dogra MBE and U. Dogra. The Sikh

World: an encyclopaedic survey of Sikh religion and culture. New Delhi, UBSPD, 2003.

Panj Takhts : Golden Temple/ Hari Mandar or Harmandir Sahib (Darbar Sahib), and its programme during day and night.

The time of opening the main gate (Darshani Deori) of the temple varies from 2am in mid-summer to 3 am in mid-winter. The gate remains closed from about four to five hours at night and is opened about three hours before sunrise. Before the opening of the main gate visitors gather and sing Sukhmani Sahib (palms of bliss) of Guru Arjan. The gate opens and the devotees enter the temple and make offerings of sweets, money and flowers and sit down to listen to the hymns being sung in the temple. This is the first shift of Ragis (musicians) who begins to sing hymns just as the gate opens. The singing goes on for an hour. After that second shift of singers arrive and sing Asa Di Var (morning prayer) of Guru Nanak and Guru Angad. At 5am the hymns stop and the Holy Granth Sahib is brought on a golden planquin-procession from the Akal Takht, where it was taken the previous night. At the gate of the temple the head priest places the Holy Granth on his head and brings it to thee already prepared seat. The priest unwraps clothes in which the Guru Granth Sahib is placed. During this ceremony hymns are sung in praise of the first five Gurus. After the priest open the Granth Sahib at random and reads from the top of the left hand page and tells the meaning of the verses to the congregation.

At 6.30 am the recitation of Asa Di Var is completed and all present stand up for Ardas (formal prayer) of the day. After the prayer ever person sits down and the priest again reads out the same lines as when the Holy Granth was first opened at random. Names of people are read out who have contributed the daily distribution of parshad (consecrated food). Parshad is distributed to the congregation in the morning and afternoon. Now the third shift of ragis (musicians) arrives and starts kirtan (singing of hymns) from the Holy book and in this way the shifts of one-and-a-half hour each continue until noon when the second prayer is said by the priest. After that the Parshad is distributed and a general cleaning of the temple takes place. Subsequent shift of musicians continue singing hymns until 5.30 pm when Sodar Ras (hymns) and Arti (evening prayers) are recited in chorus.

The singing of the hymns from the Guru Granth Sahib continues until 9.30pm when the verses are read from the bottom of the left hand of the page opened at random at 5am. The priest on duty recites Kirtan Sohela (the obligatory prayer) before retiring for the night. He closes and ceremonially wraps up the Holy Granth in many beautiful small clothes called Romalas. After that all those present rise in their seats for the final prayer. After the prayer the golden planquin arrives from the Akal Takht. The Head priest places the Holy Granth (book) on the planquin, and carries on his head the planquin to the Akal Takht, with trumpeters and conch-blowers in the lead. After this ceremony the Holy Guru Granth Sahib stays in the Akal Takht until the next morning and the main gate (Darshani Deori) is closed. Now the carpets and sheets in the temple are removed and new ones are spread. By this time it is nearly 3am when the morning kirtan begins by the first shift of musicians. It is a regular routine at the Golden Temple, but on festivals like Diwali, Baisaskhi, on the first day of every Bikrami month, on the birth anniversaries of the ten Gurus, illuminations and fireworks display are also arranged apart from the normal routine.

Harmandir Sahib / Takht Patna Sahib

The birth place of Guru Gobind Singh. Sir Charles Wilkins gives very good description.

(For more information SEE:—Sikhs and Sir Charles Wilkins – Gurdwara at Patna. IN R. C. Dogra MBE and U. Dogra. The Sikh world: an encyclopaedic survey of Sikh religion and culture. New Delhi, UBSPD, 2003. p.412-14.

Hazur Sahib also known as Abchal Nagar

This shrine is on the bank of Godavari river at Nander

(Maharashtra). The shrine is sacred to the memory of Guru Gobind Singh, who expired here on 7 October 1708. Before his death, the Guru bowed to the Guru Granth Sahib and declared it as the permanent Guru of the Sikhs. The Guru named this place Abchal Nagar (stable or unshakable place). The Gurdwara at Hazur Sahib is called Sach-Khand, which is a two-storied building, resembling the Golden Temple of Amritsar. The inside room called Angitha Sahib, where Guru Gobind Singh was actually cremated. This shrine is among the five Takhts (seats of authority for the Sikhs), and was decorated with marble and golden plate by Maharaja Ranjit Singh.

Hem-Kund/Hem-Kunt

Literally it means the pool/lake of snow. The place is situated at a level of over 17,000 feet in the Himalayas in Uttar Pradesh. Guru Gobind Singh mentioned in his autobiography that he meditated on the spot (Hem-Kund) in his previous birth. The Sikhs traced this place and Bhai Vir Singh confirmed the authenticity of the site. A Gurdwara was built there and every year Sikhs go to visit Hem-Kund. Pilgrims visit the Gurdwara and take a path in the snowy waters of the lake. Pilgrim centres like Badrinath and Gangotri are located in the nearby mountains.

Keshgarh Sahib

This is the shrine where Guru Gobind Das created the Khalsa or saint soldiers. On 30 March 1699, the Guru gave a call to Sikhs in a huge congregation, asking them to come forward to sacrifice their lives for fighting against tyranny and injustice. Five Sikhs responded to his call, and were given the new baptism (Khande-di-Pahul). They were called Panj Payaras (Beloved Five) and received Amrit from the hands of the Tenth Guru. Thereafter, the Guru himself begged of them to administer Amrit to him in the same manner as he has done to them. After taking Amrit, his name was changed from Gobind Das to Gobind Singh.

There is a magnificent Gurdwara built there, called Keshgarh Sahib. The shrine contains several weapons of the Guru. An annual fair is held on Baisakhi day at this place.

Khadur Sahib

It is very close to Goindwal (near Tarantaran) where Guru Angad (2nd Guru) propagated the message of God for many years. He heard Guru Nanak there and was selected by Guru Nanak as his successor. A Gurdwara was built at the site where Guru Angad was ceremated in Khadur.

Kirartpur Sahib

It is near Anandpur Sahib, on the banks of the Sutlej river. Guru Nanak visited the place and Guru Hargobind founded the village. The seventh and the eighth Guru were appointed in Kiratpur. . Guru Hargobind and Guru Har Rai died in Kiratpur. Kiratpur has several Gurdwaras and all of them are much revered as they are connected with the Gurus.

Majnu-ka-Tila

When Guru Nanak visited Delhi, he met a holy man on the river of river Yamuna. He was nicknamed Majnu, as he was in search of a spiritual bride. He sought the blessing of Guru Nanak and obtained enlightenment. Many holy men (Hindus and Muslims) came here for discussing their spiritual problems with the Guru. The Emperor Jahangir invited Guru Hargobind to Delhi and the Guru stayed at this place and delivered sermons to his followers. A Gurdwara erected there is sacred to the memory of Guru Nanak and Guru Hargobind. An annual summer festivals is here and many people visit the Gurdwara.

Moti Bagh Gurdwara, New Delhi

Guru Gobind Singh visited the place in 1707 when he was going to Deccan to meet Emperor Aurangzeb. On hearing the news of the death of Emperor he changed his plans and came to Delhi. Prince Muzzam, son of Aurangzeb, who later became

Emperor Bahadur Shah, received the Guru's help in gaining the throne. It is said that the Guru originally announced his arrival at the place called Moti Bagh by shooting an arrow right into the Red Fort where Emperor Bahadur Shah was staying. The Emperor took this for a miracle when a second arrow came from Guru Gobind Singh with a note that this was not a miracle but a skill in archery. A beautiful Gurdwara is built there, called Moti Bagh Gurdwara.

Panja Sahib

On his return from a tour of the Middle East, Guru Nanak halted at Hasan Abdul (about 48 kms from Rawalpindi) at the foot of a hill. Here lived a Muslim holy man called Wali Khandari on the top of the hill. Mardana felt thirsty and Guru Nanak told him to go up the hill to get some drinking water. Twice the Muslim fakir (holy man) refused to give him any water to drink. Nanak dug up the earth and a spring sprang forth from the spot. It soon appeared that the holy man's pool was drained. In anger, the holy man rolled a boulder towards the Guru sitting at the foot of the hill. The Guru stopped the huge stone with his hand, and the imprint of his palm got engraved on the stone. Panja means the five fingers of the hand. The Muslim holy man felt repentant and apologised to the Guru for his indiscretion. He became an admirer of the Guru, and turned a new leaf in his life. A huge Gurdwara is built there and many people from different countries visit the Gurdwara at Panja Sahib in Pakistan.

Paonta Sahib

Paonta Sahib is a beautiful spot in Nahan district (Himachal Pradesh). It is about 80 miles to the northeast of Ambala. Guru Gobind Singh came here in 1684, and built a fort on the bank of river Yamuna. The presence of the Guru brought peace between the rival Rajas. A magnificent Gurdwara was built on the bank of river Yamuna. Many people visit the Gurdwara every year.

Rakabganj Sahib

Literallt Rakabganj means a place for the storage of stirrups. During Mughal times the place was used for the king's bodyguards and stables. At this spot Bhai Lakhi Shah Labhana cremated the body of Guru Tegh Bahadur on the night of 11 November 1675. Sardar Baghel Singh built a Gurdwara there in the memory of Guru Tegh Bahadur. A new marble building has recently been built, decorated by several domes. A Sikh missionary school is being run on the premises. A few weapons of Guru Gobind Singh are preserved in the Gurdwara. The Delhi Gurdwara Management Committee, under an Act of Parliament, manages it.

Taran Taran Sahib

It is near Amritsar where Guru Arjan Dev built a Gurdwara in the memory of Guru Ram Das. Taran Taran is famous for its tank, the water of which is said to cure leprosy.

Panj Takhts

Panj Takht means the five centres/seats of Sikh authority. These are connected with certain important events in the lives of the Gurus. These are: (1) The Akal Takht built by Guru Hargobind to indicate the twin doctrine of Miri and Piri. (2) Takht Patna Sahib, Patna. (3) Takht Keshgarh Sahib, the place of creation of the Khalsa at Anandpur (1699). (4) Takht Sri Hazur Sahib (Nander) where Guru Gobind Singh was cremated. (5) Takht Sri Damdama Sahib (Panjab) where Guru Gobind Singh dictated the final version of the Adi Granth. The head of the Takht is called Jathedar, and he has the authority to issue Hukamnamas (religious edicts), which are binding for all

Sikhism—its connection with monotheism and polytheism

It is well known that on the one hand Sikhism has its source in a movement within Hinduism, and on the other it is presumed that it owes something to Vedas. The doctrine of the one Supreme God, as proclaimed by Nanak had always been present within Hinduism. The saints and reformers who preceded the Sikh Gurus, and to whom the later were so much indebted for the very phrases used in their hymns, were mostly Hindus, if Muslim, had been largely influenced by Hinduism. Their declaration of the Unity of Gods was part of a natural Hindu development. Ramanuja (1017-1137), Tamil Brahmin philosopher, grandson of a famous Vaishnava high priest of South India, taught that the Supreme Deity (may be referred as Brahma, Ishvar or Vishnu) is the cause and creator of all things. He is eternally free from all imperfections, and apart from the Supreme deity (Brahma/Ishvara) there is nothing. The Supreme spirit/Brahma is full of love and pity for mankind, and sometimes it becomes incarnate for the salvation of men e.g. Ram or Krishna. Ramanuja taught that the individual soul is subject to ignorance and suffering, and the means of salvation is not knowledge but faith (bhakti) meditation on the name of God. He influenced Madhava, Vallabha, Chaitanya Ramananada, Kabir, Guru Nanak, Brahmo Samaj and other reform movements.

Monotheistic thought has grown from Polytheism of Hindus. From the very earliest times in the Rig Veda a tendency to monotheism may be noticed. One God is frequently chosen from the rest of the pantheon and exalted in some particular hymn till he becomes supreme and infinite, all lesser deities being his inferior and emanations from him. The acknowledgement of some such secondary beings in no way conflicts with monotheistic doctrine, for in Catholic Christendom or in the existence of saints, angels and archangels is admitted and other sects of Islam (Ahmadiya, Sunnites, Zaydites and other reform movements) propagated their own beliefs. This tendency to raise first one god and then another to the position of Supreme Deity gradually gained ground, but later out of the more general polytheism of the Vedas a mystical and subtle philosophy arose, which God became the neuter World-Soul, immanent in matter. He thus lost the attributes of personality and could only be expressed by negation and realised by meditation. The belief in monotheism or in the personality of God and in the possibility of approaching Him with prayer and devotion. These movements frequently arose in the warrior caste and they asserted the rights of the laity as against those of the priesthood. It is true that monotheistic doctrine had never been absent from Hinduism, though it belonged less to orthodoxy than to particular movements of reform. The Hindu Bhagat or saints, who preceded Nanak, show to a considerable extent this influence of monotheistic devotion, which developed, from Hinduism. No doubt that Hindu reformers like Kabir, Guru Nanak, protested against idolatry, formality, and caste system, but in practice they did not break away from their parent religion i.e. Hinduism.

The fact that Guru Nanak was originally very friendly to the Muhammadans was soon forgotten; bitterness arose between the followers of the two religions, persecution of Sikhs and Hindus being largely accountable for the magnificent martial development of the other. Guru Nanak did reject certain features of Hinduism, but his doctrine concern God, His nature and attributes, and man, and the means by which salvation may be attained were influenced by the doctrines of the saints preceded him. There are three aspects under which the nature of God has been conceived. In the first He is omnipotent Being, Ruler and Creator of the world, the Father and Judge of men. In the second He becomes incarnate for the salvation of mankind or is specially manifested in some teacher or Guru. In the third he is immanent spirit, the Life and Soul of all that is.

All these things were in Hinduism in one form or the other.

The philosophy of the Gurus does not escape polytheism as it practically assumes the Hindu pantheon and mythology. It accepts the doctrine of Karma, transmigration, repetition of the name, necessity of the guru, Bhakti (salvation by grace for all), Maya (world—God's play), salvation by death in battle (found in 10th Granth as mentioned in the Bhagvad Gita). The keynote of the Guru's instruction was greater simplicity in belief and worship. Guru Nanak propagated in repetition of God's name. The custom of repeating a sacred name was already an inherent factor of Hindu religion, and many worshippers of Krishna repeat his name thousands of times daily. The Guru approved the practice, but he substituted a new name for God (Ek Omkar sat nam—one God true name). Guru Nanak wants his follower to repeat the name of such a God who is ever true.

The teaching of the Sikhs owes much to Kabir. The Sikhism believes in one God and He is the True Name. Sikhism dropped many Hindu features but adopted many similar features in disguised form, e.g. set aside the authority of the Vedas, but substituted for it the authority of the Guru Granth Sahib. Nanak is regarded as an incarnation of God, possessing the sixteen incarnation signs of Ram and Krishna. It is known that Nanak performed miracles, cleansed lepers, and raised the dead. The other Gurus are regarded as an incarnation of Nanak, assuming his divinity upon their formal installation . Sikhism prohibit idolatry, but they themselves pay the same idolatrous homage to the Guru Granth Sahib, photographs of all the Gurus are hung on walls in all the Gurudwaras of the world; they are not supposed to observe class distinction, but they are greatly influenced by caste system and many bear caste names. Smoking, drinking of wine and drugs are prohibited, but many Sikhs do take liquor and Nihangs take hemp in liquid form. Namdhari Sikhs (Kukas) do not eat meat, drink spirits or take hemp or smoke tabacco. Another sect of the Sikhs, Nanakpanthis, are a religious and non-political sect of the Sikhs, they follow the teachings of Guru Nanak, but do not believe in all the teachings of Guru Gobind Singh. They do not keep long hairs and are not distinguishable from the Hindus. Pilgrimage to holy places is forbidden, but pilgrimage to Amritsar is religious duty of every Sikh. Similar to Hinduism the Sikh Gurus recommended Ahinsa (non-injury to life) in thought, word and deed. Sikhism is a synthesis of Kabir, Ramanuja and other reform movements in Hinduism.

Guru Nanak had all the reformative tendencies of Hindu reformers but he associated with them a greater amount of authority than had any of previous reformers.)

Hindu-Sikh relations

All the great religions of the world may be regarded as universal in spirit. Some of them were founded by the individual prophets, but the Hinduism was revealed to a number of sages. Buddhism, Christianity and Islam are religions founded by individuals. Hinduism has no single founder; the ancient sages served as channels for the transmission of religious truths to humanity. Sikhs are a religious sect, followers of Guru Nanak (1469-1539). They have always been respected members of Hindu society. Hindus at large have always respected reform movements in Hinduism. There has always been inter-marriage, common food and other common things between the Hindu and the Sikh communities. Guru Nanak was the Guru or preceptor of both Hindus and Sikhs. He was a part of the Bhakti movement—devotion, dedication, and love of God to his creatures and of a human being to God. A devotee clings to his God in his need for divine love and protection and God carries his faithful believer lovingly towards a safe and protected life. The doctrine of Bhakti was an important innovation upon the old Vedic religion. In the Bhagavad-Gita (the song of the Divine One) Lord Krishna says that Bhakti (worship or remembering the Holy Name) is infinitely more efficacious than any or all observances. In the religious sects started by Chaitanya Mahaprabhu (Hare Krishna movment), Kabir and Guru Nanak etc., all persons of all castes are admitted into their sects or religion, and they tried to convey their bhakti message through devotional songs.

Guru Nanak's followers were called Sikh/Sikhs (a Sanskrit word meaning a disciple or learner) Like Hindus, the Guru considered the consumption of flesh and wine unlawful. Ramanuja (1017-1137) taught equality of races, abolition of caste system. His influence may be discerned in the works of later reformers e.g. Madhva, Vallabha, Chaitanya, Ramananada, Kabir, Guru Nanak, and the reform Brahmo Samaj movement. Guru Nanak realised the Divine presence in all people and so valued every human life. The most important feature in the ideology of Guru Nanak was the concept of God and man's relations with him. The concept of Guru changed than the conception of God in the compositions of Guru Nanak's successors. Guru Angad (2nd. Guru) thought that God, hymns (Shabad) and the Guru were very important for salvation. For Guru Amardas (3rd Guru) there was only one true Guru and those who do not serve Him—remain in misery. For Guru Ramdas (4th Guru), the Guru was everything (father, mother, relation, friend). Guru Arjun (5th Guru) believed that the Guru was the King of Kings and is the true Guru, the God (Par-Brahm, Niranjan). The ideas of Guru Nanak to reform Hinduism were re-enforced by his successors who were known as Nanak the first, second, third, fourth and so on.

Hinduism believed both in monotheism and polytheism. Guru Nanak accepted the monotheism of the Hindus. He believed that God was immortal. The ideal of Guru-ship was well established in Hinduism, and Guru Nanak laid down its foundation of a living faith. The succession of Guru-ship was not unknown in Hinduism, but Guru Nanak added a new feature; it meant that the succeeding Gurus became the incarnation of the founder. One of the major beliefs in Hinduism is the incarnation theory. Before Nanak died he transmitted his Guru-ship to Lahna (1504-1552), named Angad (own body), by a simple Hindu ceremony. Guru Nanak laid five paisa coin and a coconut before Angad (Khatri Hindu), went four times round his successor and then said that his own spirit had gone into his body so that he was from that moment to be regarded as Nanak the second. This event occurred in 1537 AD. The successive Gurus transmitted their office by this rite. Bhai Buddha, a Jat, affixed the tilak of coronation mark on Angad's forehead and survived to witness the installation of no less than four of Angad's successor's in the same way. He was succeeded by Amar Das (meaning immortal devotee). Amar Das transmitted Guru ship to his son-in-law Guru Ram Das (meaning devotee of Lord Ram). From that time onwards the Guru ship remained within the family.

Guru Ram Das built Harimandar (temple of God Hari). (Hari is an epithet used for several Gods, e.g. Indra, Shiva, Vishnu, but Lord Vishnu in particular is known by the name of Hari). All the names of these Gurus are connected with Hinduism and Hindu mythology.

The fourth Mughal emperor Jahangir (1605-1627) ascended the throne with the help of fanatic Muslims; he martyred the fifth Guru (Arjun Dev). Hindus mourned and Muslims enjoyed the downfall of the Guru. Guru Tegh Bahadur was called Pir (saint) of Hindus by the Emperor Aurangzeb. Guru Tegh Bahadur decided to stand up for the right of freedom of worship and told the Emperor that he was ready to sacrifice his life to protect Hindus from mass conversion to Islam. The teachings and glories of the Sikh Gurus are also glories of the Hindus. Hindus and Sikhs are of the same blood, history, aspiration and interest. From the time of Guru Gobind Singh the eldest son born in a Hindu family was made to become a Sikh (in order to enlist later in the community of saint warriors). The saint warrior believed in Dharam-Yudh (war of righteousness) for securing freedom and justice. Guru Hargobind (6th Guru) raised an army to fight against Mughal oppression and injustice. Guru Gobind Singh (10th Guru) amplified the Hindu/Sikh concept of Dharam-yudh as known in the story of the Mahabharata, which no doubt had a basis of fact in the old Hindu traditions.

The tenth and the last Guru Gobind Rai, later Gobind Singh was surrounded during his childhood by Hindu influences. Gobind Rai succeeded to his office under every temptation to remain within the pale of orthodox Hinduism, and indeed one tradition asserts that his first act was to ascend to the temple of Naina Devi, which stands, on a precipitous hill overlooking the Sutlej River. The story goes that Guru Gobind before embarking on his campaign against the Turks sought the aid of the Goddess Naina Devi. With the help of a Brahman of Benares he kept up for months the Homa (Yajna) rite for the propitiation of the Goddess Durga, so that she might appear and bless the new Khalsa sect, and they also preached the power of the goddess, persuading the Sikhs to make offerings and sacrifices to her in order to obtain invincibility. At last the Devi appeared and the Guru awe-stricken, presented his sword which she touched and disappeared. (H.A. Rose. A glossary of the tribes and castes of the Punjab. Lahore, 1919. Vol.1. P. 694-95).

Bir Singh, in a letter to Khalsa Akhbar (12 February 1897) refers to a picture of the Goddess Durga painted on the front wall of a room near the Dukhbhanjani Beri, in the Golden temple (Amritsar) precincts. He says that the Goddess stands on golden sandals and has many hands. One of the hands is stretched out and in this she holds a Khanda. Guru Gobind Singh stands before it with his folded hands.

Guru Gobind Singh wrote on many subjects including Goddess Chandi and her wonders. It is based on Markande Puran, and is in Hindi. The Guru also wrote on the Hindu incarnations of Lord Vishnu. The importance of the writings of the Guru lies first, in its being a source of material on the life and mission of the Guru, Indian history, folklore and culture; a treasure of lyrical poetry; thirdly, a typical collection of literature in Hindi, Panjabi, and Persian of that period. Dasam Granth is not read in Gurudwaras, but a complete reading of the Dasam Granth is held on certain Sikh festivals at Takht Sri Hazur Sahib, Nanded (Maharashtra); none of the writings of the Guru are included in the Guru Granth Sahib, the holy book of the Sikhs.

The Dasam Granth of Guru Gobind Singh consist of divine prayers, tales of heroism, from ancient Hindu literature of old sages, saints, and seers. The Guru's composition is in Hindi (Awadhi and Brajbhasha), except the concluding portion, the language of which is Persian and includes some Arabic words. The Granth reveals the national spirit, and heroic stories of Hindu ancestors. Most of the characters are from Puranic stories. The freedom fighters are praised who fought against tyranny and oppression. All the stories in the Granth are full of patriotism and nationalism.

On Baisakhi day (30 March) in 1999 Hindus and Sikhs celebrated the 300th Baisakhi marking of the birth of Khalsa (pure). These celebrations in India and all over the world demonstrated the growth of the Sikh community with its rich culture and traditions, playing a positive role in the life of the Hindu/Sikh community in India and abroad. The ceremony of Baptism (Pahul), established by Guru Nanak is called Charan Ghawal and consisted in the drinking of water touched by the Guru's toe. It is the same as the Hindu ceremony. Though it is seldom used, but still exists between the Sahajdhari and Nanak Panthi Sikhs. The last Guru Gobind Singh changed it and started a new ceremony (Khande-de-Pahul—water stirred with double-edged sword) on 30 March 1699. All his followers were given the name of Singh. The Guru made an appeal in the name of the country and nation; great emphasis on the love of motherland and loyalty to dharma. He dwelt on the necessity of subverting the Mughal Empire and building a new nation. The creation of the Khalsa was an epoch-making event in the history of India. It marked the beginning of the rise of new people against tyrannical despotism of Aurangzeb. Under the direction or 10th Guru, the Khalsa took up the arms and the results were encouraging.

Sikh-Muslim relations during the time of Sikh Gurus (1469-1708)

Guru Nanak tells us that in his days the kings had become butchers and cannibals, official dogs licked the blood and devoured the flesh of the people in their power; there was none to protect the honour of the weak, Hindus and women. All was falsehood, and religion had flown away from horrors as it beheld when Babar came to India. Most people sunk under the burden of misery into a pessimistic resignation, but it stung Nanak into even challenging God for tolerating such brutalities (Asa Ki war 39: 1-2). During the Guru's travels he wore a strange mixture of Hindu and Muslim costumes. This is supposed to show that he did not regard the two religions as essentially opposed in their pure forms, and that his own teachings might be acceptable to Muslims as well. It is said that during the time of Guru Amardas, 3rd. Guru (1552-1574) emperor Akbar visited the Guru at Goindwal and gave him a grant of some villages around the present city of Amritsar. The emperor's visit greatly enhanced the prestige and financial position of the Guru. The emperor Akbar also visited Guru Arjan (1581-1606), and on his request remitted the revenues of the Panjab for one year. Akbar's friendliness to the Gurus was a great help to their fame and prestige. Of Nanak's life few authentic details have come down to us from his Janamsakhis (biographies), which at least record the traditional attitude of the earlier Hinduism/Sikhism to Islam. Thus immediately after Nanak's election for a spiritual life he is said to have been visited by Khwaja Khizr, the Muhammadan saint, who taught him some earthly knowledge. The traditional account of Guru Nanak's funeral also records his attitude towards the Hindu/Muslim religions. When the Hindus and the Muhammadans both claimed his body he bade them lay flowers on either side of it, for Hindus on the right and for Muslims on the left, hiding them see whose flowers remains fresh till the following day. But next morning both lots of flowers were found fresh, while the body had vanished, signifying that it belonged to neither, yet equally to both the religions.

During the time of Guru Nanak Hindus were divided over petty dynastic and personal quarrels, the people of India put up a very poor defence against the ruthless and terrible invaders from the Muslim Middle-East. In each province of India a few battles, a few secret betrayals were enough to replace Indian rulers by Muslim rulers, temples by mosques, Hindu religious books by the Quran. Inspite of humiliation and persecution many Hindus retained their religion at a price, and under the Muslim kings lived lives of slaves. Many Hindus died who did not embrace Islam; millions of Hindus embraced Islam to avoid persecution and death. Where the local Muslim authorities were tolerant, Hindus were allowed to worship and perform their pilgrimages. Many Hindus found it useful, while in their hearts keeping alive their Hindu religion, to conform outwardly with that of the Muslim, adopting Muslim dress, even attending the mosques and repeating the Muslim creed in public, so as to secure immunity from poll-tax and persecution alike, and open the door to their own social and financial advancement—for it was all but impossible for a loyal Hindus to gain worthy employment at that time or to hold a job in the court. It was an unhappy time for the Hindus.

The Muslim king at Delhi cared little or nothing for the welfare of Hindus; most of them held that Hindus were created to be the slaves of Muslim believers and their family might be broken up to satisfy the demands of lust. Nor did things improve under the Mughal rule. Rulers taxation on Hindus, the farming out of all lands to contractors who fleeced the people to the utmost, so as to get enough for their own survival the people bribed the officials and secured the privilege for the future corruption. The were a prey to brutal murderers and dacoits; desolated by cruelty, wastefulness and vice—honours and places freely bought and sold, the rulers sunk in luxury and vicious debauchery. Some rulers excessively intolerant and fanatical, to such an extent that they would allow Hindus to keep only enough corn and coarse cloth for six months; the common people and their Mullahs were ignorant of their own religion by ignoring both the principles of the Quran and all the humane laws of the Shariat. They believed that non-Muslims were solely for their own pleasure as slaves. Some Muslim saints were very successful in converting Hindus into Islam as they imitated the Hindus in withdrawing from society for the most part into the forests, where they could live in peace undisturbed by the cruelties which devastated India.

Muslims looked upon all women as playthings for their own lusts, as little better than toys or animals; intense distrust of them made them imprison them in rooms away from sunlight and fresh air, letting them go out only under escort and disfigured with the hideous black veil (Burka). When a daughter was born to a family it was looked upon as a dreadful calamity, so infanticide, strictly forbidden by the Quran, became quite common among Muslims. It is said that even Sati was not unknown among them in the days of Jahangirt. Such is the picture of the life Hindu/Sikh lived at the time of Gurus.

Guru Arjan's activity (1563-1606) was not confined to spiritual affairs. He also established the beginnings of a fiscal system, appointing collectors, called Masands, to each of whom was assigned a definite district. With the vigour and initiative of Arjan's leadership the Hindus/Sikhs were rising in importance, and since they now possessed both a sacred volume (Guru Granth Sahib), and a sacred city (Amritsar), the attention of the of suspicious and fanatical emperor Jahangir was directed towards him. This ruler, believing Guru Arjan to be involved in political rebellion against him, summoned him to his court. There the complaints against sacred volume were renewed, and Arjan was ordered to erase all passages that were supposed to reflect on Muhammadan doctrine. He refused to do, and on refusing to submit, the Guru was subjected to terrible torture. Indeed the Dabistan, which contains the most probable account of Guru Arjan's death, says he was accused, like many other Panjab notables, of actual participation in Prince Khusrau's rebellion. It is certain that Jahangir condemned him to a heavy fine. Unable or unwilling to pay the sum demanded he was exposed to the sun's rays and was also subjected to terrible tortures. He died in 1606 as the result of this treatment.

Arjan's son Hargobind (1595-1644) succeeded to the Guru ship. He was the first Guru to take up arms against the Muhammadans to whom he certainly ascribed his father's death. He built the stronghold of Hargovindpur on the upper reaches of the Beas to attack the rulers. To protect the young community of disciples already subject to persecution, the sixth Guru converted it into a semi-military brotherhood, arming it with outward insignia and sacraments, and thus subjecting it to the purifying fires of martyrdom, which instilled the necessary courage and manly resolution in its heart. To his standard flocked many whom want and misgovernment had driven from their homes. But at last the Guru fell into the hands of the imperial troops, and Jahangir kept him a prisoner at Gwalior for twelve years, until in 1628, on that emperor's death, he obtained his freedom by sacrificing his treasures. Returning to Kiratpur the Guru renewed his attacks on the Muhammadan landowners and imperial officials of the plains.

On Guru Hargobind's death at Kiratpur in 1644 his grandson Har Rai succeeded him. His alliance was successfully sought by another rebellious scion of the Mughal house, Dara Shikoh, who soon perished. Therefore the Guru retreated to Kiratpur when he sent his son Ram Rao to Delhi to negotiate pardon. Aurangzeb received the young envoy graciously, but detained him as a hostage for his father's loyalty. Har Rai contributed not a single verse to the Guru Granth Sahib. He died in 1661 at Kiratpur and his second son a minor (Har Krishan) the 8th Guru succeeded him. Ram Rai still a hostage, appealed to Aurangzeb, who seized the pretext for interference in the Guru's domestic affairs and summoned Har Krishan to Delhi. There he died of smallpox at the age of eight.

In 1664 Guru Tegh Bahadur (1665-1674) obtained recognition as the 9th Guru. He was a great figure who founded Anandpur in 1665. Still harassed by Aurangzeb and his opponents the Guru set out on a progress through the Malwa country—a tract full of shrines, tanks, and Dharamsalas (rest houses) which commemorates his visits.

About this time Aurangzeb was carrying on a bitter persecution of the Hindus. The Hindus complained to the Guru that Aurangzeb was destroying their religion by force, burning down temples, breaking images, and ill-treating the worshippers. In his attempt to Muhammadan India he had excited grave opposition and Guru Tegh Bahadur recognised if Guru Nanak's acquiescence in the Muslim sovereignty was to be revoked his own life must be the price of the revocation. Accordingly he sent the Kashmiri Pandits who had appealed to him in their distress to make a petition to the emperor

Aurangzeb in these words:- "We live on the offerings of the Kshatriyas. Guru Tegh Bahadur, the foremost among them, is now seated on the throne of Guru Nanak and is Guru of all the Hindus. If you could first make him a Mussalman, then all the Sikhs and Brahmans who follow him will of their own accord adopt your faith". The emperor accordingly summoned the Guru to Delhi and he replied that he would come after the rains. That season he passed at Saifabad with Saif-ud-Din his devotee, and went to Delhi with his five followers. There he was seized and resisting every inducement to forsake his faith was eventually put to death. He sent a dying message to his son Gobind Rai to stay fearlessly in Anandpur. On receiving this message Gobind Rai, a boy of nine left Lakhnaur and from there he went to stay at Anandpur with his mother.

Guru Gobind Rai (later became Guru Gobind Singh, the word Singh was added to his name only nine years before his death), was, however, bitterly opposed to Islam. The execution of his father called for retribution, and the Guru instituted the Pahul or rite of initiation in 1699, whereby all Hindus were admitted into a sacred brotherhood of Khalsa (pure). It was an army of saint-warriors who would always be armed to defend their rights, to seek justice and to stop the conversion of Hindus to Islam. Saint-warriors always wore blue clothes, worn by Lord Krishna and his elder brother Balram. Guru Gobind Singh died in 1708; a year after Aurangzeb had died in 1707.

His disciple Banda Bahadur as military commander of the Khalsa succeeded Guru Gobind Singh. Banda proceeded to wage open and relentless war on all Muslims. He exacted vengeance for the execution of Guru Tegh Bahadur, and for the treachery of the Pathans at Damla. He killed personally Nawab Wazir Khan of Sarhind who bricked alive two younger sons (Zorawar Singh and Fateh Singh) of the Guru as they refused to become Muslims. In 1712 he occupied Sirhand and the Rajas of Sirmur, Nalagarh and Bilaspur also submitted to his allegiance. He reduced the Muhammadan Jagirdars of

Rupar, Bssi, Kiri and Bahlolpur to a similar position, and in 1714 he was strong enough to hold a regal darbar (court) at Amritsar at which he appeared in royal dress with an aigrette on his head.

In 1713 Farrukhsiar's reign began and he promptly attacked the Sikhs on two sides, but Banda and his army drove back the imperials thus bringing the country between Lahore and Jammu under the Sikh rule before Ranjit Singh. In order to weaken the Sikhs Farrukhsiar hatched a plan and was successful in dividing the Sikhs by using the influence of Guru Gobind Singh's widow against Banda, who was excommunicated on eight counts in that he had married, started a new creed, substituted a charan pahul (baptism) for the Sikh Khanda de pahul (baptism), invented the war cry of Fatah Darasan (victory of the faith), attired himself in royal robes, styled himself the 11th Guru and claimed to rule the Sikhs, his followers being called Bandai Sikhs instead of the Singhs of the Guru. Banda's answer to these charges was significant. He said he was merely a Bairagi faqir (holy man) and a follower of the Guru in his mission to destroy the Mughals. He was merely carrying out his orders to conquer Panjab, punish those who have put to death Guru Tegh Bahadur, two minor sons of Guru Gobind Singh, and the protection of the Khalsa. The army was divided into Tat Khalsa and Bandai Sikhs. All his efforts at reconciliation with the Tat Khalsa failed and in 1716 he was captured at the siege of Gurdaspur and put to death with great cruelty.

After Banda's execution the Sikhs waged implacable war against the Muslim rulers, but made no attempt to establish an organised government until Ranjit Singh, Maharaja of Panjab.

It is well known that the fight of the Gurus was against the Muslim rulers and not ordinary Muslims, therefore many Muslims became devotees of Gurus and some Muslim vocabulary is also found in the Guru Granth Sahib.

Mohsin Fani (a great traveller in India, and his views on Sikh Gurus)

He was the author of Dabistan-e Mazhib, a great scholarly and factual book on Sikh Gurus and India. He was a contemporary of the fifth (Guru Arjan), sixth (Guru Hargobind) and seventh Guru (Guru Har Rai). He spent fifteen year in Panjab and was very friendly with the Gurus. He was a great friend of Guru Hargobind and was present at the time of his death at Kiratpur. His work (Dabistan-e Mazhib) is very valuable for honest and truthful observations about the Sikh Gurus and India. In Dabistan-e Mazhib the following information is found about the Gurus:

1. The Sikhs believe that all the Gurus are incarnation of Guru Nanak.
2. The Guru's Masands (tax collectors) are Jats.
3. The Sikhs call their Gurus—Sache Padshah (true monarch) and their agents are called Masands.
4. The Emperor Jahangir, eldest son of the Emperor Akbar, succeeded his father in 1605. His eldest son Khusrau rebelled against his father and while he was passing through Lahore, he was blessed by Guru Arjan Mal by putting a red mark of victory on his head. After the capture of Khusrau the Emperor for blessing Khusrau fined the Guru. The Guru could not pay the fine. He was kept in prison in Lahore. He died of torture by the prison authorities.
5. The emperor did not like the sixth Guru Hargobind and asked him to pay the fine, which had been imposed on his father Guru Arjan Mal. Guru Hargobind was also sent to Gwalior prison for twelve years for not paying the fine.
6. During this time Masands and devotees used to go to prison and bow before the walls of the prison fort at Gwalior. The emperor released the Guru and he reached Amritsar on the eve of Diwali day and the devotees illuminated the Golden Temple and the city in his honour to celebrate Diwali.

7. The Guru returned to Amritsar where Guru Ram Das and Arjan Mal had erected beautiful buildings and a beautiful tank. There he was attacked by the army of imperial officials under orders of Shah Jahan, and the Guru's property was plundered. He left Amritsar and went to Kartarpur where he has to fight a battle with Muslims and cut off the head of a man with one stroke who had threatened him.
8. After the battle he went to Phagwara and from there he went to Kiratpur for his safety.
9. Guru Hargobind had 700 horses in his stable, and 300 mounted troopers and 60 gunners were always n his service. He gave shelter to every one and even fugitives.
10. When Guru Hargobind died, his personal servant (Raja Ram) and another devotee jumped on his funeral pyre. After that devotees were not allowed to jump on his funeral pyre to commit suicide.
11. Guru Har Rai stayed at Kiratpur for one year and then went to stay at Nahan in the territory of Raja Karan Prakash. He felt safe at Nahan from the Muslim rulers of Delhi.

12. Sikhs calls Guru Har Rai Mohalla Seventh. He is a great frined of the author (Mohsin Fani)

Sikh family life

Family life is very important to Sikhs to maintain their simplicity and pride. Girls are given good education, as far as possible, and are also made to learn household skills. Mealtimes are family occasions and are enjoyed properly. The Sikhs are told by the Gurus to be vegetarian, except the last Guru (Guru Gobind Singh) who told them to eat meat if vegetarian food is not available. In order to demonstrate their difference from Muslims, they do not eat Halal meat (ritually slaughtered animals according to Islam). Home and Gurdwaras are the places for entertainment. Usually the Sikhs do not like unmarried boys and girls to go out together alone, and they prefer to meet their friends in homes or Gurdwaras. There are usually arranged marriages in villages, and the couples meet each other after marriage. In cities and towns the couples are allowed to meet and know each other before marriage. A lot of attention is paid in the selection of a husband and wife, making sure that they could afford to marry and live happily. Most of the arranged marriages are successful. In this way the Sikh families pass their customs and teachings of their religion to their children for their benefit.

Sikh/Panjabi—family relationship

The relationship rules are usually derived from local customs and nature. The marriage and procreation creates ties between the family members. It is believed that behaviour in a family is governed by nature. Sometimes the moral order is based on natural order, e.g. homosexuality or lesbian relationship is taken against local customs and human nature. Incest is also seen against nature and against the morals of the community. Human nature is known as animal in origin and natural, but the moral code is against the people behaving like animals.

The theory of procreation is that the woman provides the field and the man provides the seed. The quality of the offspring is determined by the quality of the seed and the field. They should be equally matched. The man's role ends with the depositing of the seed. The seed grows and becomes a child in mother's womb. When a woman becomes pregnant her menstruation stops and the mother keeps the child in her womb for nine months. The blood and flesh of the child is from mother's blood of menstruation and the bones of the child are formed from the semen. During this period it is important that mother observe a number of dietary taboos, eat special foods for the health of the baby, keep ritual observance and also keep her thoughts pure. The love between mother and child is natural. It is usually said that a wife is replaceable but the mother is irreplaceable. When in pain or in trouble a person always calls his mother (Haai Maan) but never his father (Haai Pita) or his wife (Haai Biwi)

For a few months or a year, when the mother is suckling the baby there are certain restrictions about the food. A good food, pious thinking and good behaviour of the mother will enable the child to become a good member of the family and society. The process of shaping the baby in the womb and nursing the child properly after the birth creates love and affection between mother and child.

The relation between a father and a child is considered less than the relation between a mother and a child. Although Khun ka khichao (pull of the blood) attracts the child to the father. If there is a fight between brothers or brothers and sisters over property is described as dogs fighting over a bone. Usually it is described Sharika pirde paiye ne. It means that some companions are fighting with each other and not blood relations. It is often stated in a Panjabi family that the love of the mother for the child is more than the child's love for the mother. After the marriage of the child the nature takes its course and the bonds created by procreation becomes less strong than the new bonds created by sexuality. The mother may not show her too much love for a son after his marriage, but it is always present. It is often said in a Panjabi family that the son may be a bad son (Kuputra) and the mother cannot be a bad mother (Kumata). The sexuality of female is protected with greater care and every effort is made to control the excessive growth of passions in young girls by telling them stories with good morals, balanced food and simple clothes. It does not mean that the sexuality of a girl is denied, but it means that the girls is told to respect the natural moral laws and do not allow promiscuity until marriage. Sexuality creates strong bonds between a husband and wife. A wife is replaceable but not mother. There can be two or more wives, but only one mother.

The ties of biological kinship are treated as more natural, and the ties of the social kinship are created by the society.

The violation of moral rules is expressed as (sharam haya nahin hai) in the idiom of shame and loss of face.

In a joint family system, in small towns and villages, a newly married couple ignore each other completely during the day. There is a great tension between the ties created by sexuality and those created by procreation, and a man is often torn between the loyalty to his mother and his wife. But the loyalty to wife is usually more after marriage and that is wife a young wife is often get accused that she has done (Jade tuna) magic spells to her husband. Sometimes the quarrel between the mother-in-law and daughter-in-law gets too bad and continue to deteriorate the young husband and wife set up a separate house. Usually the relations between the mother-in-law and daughter-in-law are hostile due to the conflict created by the ties of natural sexuality and procreation.

It is true that in a Punjabi family kinship operates at two levels i.e. biological and the social. Honourable conduct demands a sacrifice of the natural ties created by biology and kinship. Usually it is possible for the members of the family to derive the legitimacy of their conduct from honour, etiquette or natural human values.

The daughter has a special place in Panjabi families, being seen as a responsibility of family honour. Dishonourable conduct on the part of a daughter can ruin the honour of the family, leaving the parents to show their face to their relations and friends.

Usually in families inter-personal relations are conducted at two levels, i.e., (a) biological ties and (b) by etiquette and honour of the family. Etiquette and honour of the family is also expressed as duniyadari (ways of the world). Thus one has to visit relations and give gifts not for biological reasons but for duniyadari to maintain social ties. The word bhai (brother) and bahen (sister) are very commonly used. Apart from your own brother, people of the same generation always chooses the term (bhai sahib or para Ji) to a relation, stranger or the known person or a customer, even if the name is known to the caller. Similarly the word bahen (sister) is used in kinship, non-kinship and casual contexts. The term sala (brother-in-law) or jeeja (sister's husband). The term sala either used to mean privileged familiarity or an abuse.

Every possible effort is made by the family to protect their daughter or any other female member from the possibility of gossip. The parents and the brother of the girl remain the main helper and protector of the girl. The concept of honour holds a very important place in Panjabi kinship. It not only provides the link between self and community, but also between self and the idealised norms of the community.

4

Ceremonies in Sikhism

Guru Granth Sahib installation ceremony

The tenth and the last Guru, Guru Gobind Singh, instructed his followers that after him, the Holy Granth, as the voice of the Gurus, was to be respected as the Guru himself. The Holy book is kept wrapped in a fine cloth, in any room, which is reserved for praying only. An altar is improvised by placing a small bed on a wooden Divan, under a canopy. The Holy Book (Guru Granth Sahib), is brought in with all reverence. Everyone rises to acknowledge it. It is placed on the bed and its wrappings are arranged round it in a proper order, then the Holy Book is opened and read. The Sikh who opens and reads it called the Granthi, but any Sikh man or woman can perform this ceremony. Every Sikh ceremony takes place in the presence of the Guru Granth Sahib.

Baptism Ceremony (Pahul of Guru Gobind Singh on 30 March 1699) also called Khande-de-Pahul.

The ceremony of baptism established by Guru Nanak, was called Charan Ghawal and consisted in drinking of water touched by the Guru's toes. Though seldom used, it still exists between the Sahajdhari (Nanak Panthi Sikhs), who revere Nanak as their Guru in preference to Guru Gobind Singh. . Later, on 30 March 1699, Guru Gobind Singh started a new ceremony called Khande-de-Pahul (water stirred with double edged sword). When a girl or boy has reached an intelligent age (between twelve to eighteen), and is able to read the writings of the Guru or understand the teachings of the Sikh faith, pahul or baptism is administered to him or her by the Granthi (priest) in the presence of the Guru Granth Sahib.

Children who have been keeping five symbols (hair, dagger, comb, iron bangle, and breeches), in case of boys, ask permission with folded hands to be admitted to the membership of the Sikh community. Five Sikhs (Panj Payaras) who are known for their strict observance of Sikh faith are chosen to administer pahul (baptism), One of them acting as a senior brother asks if they are prepared to accept: 1. To believe in Guru Granth Sahib and recite Sikh prayers daily. (2) To keep five k's (kangha, kes, kara, kachcha, karpan). (3) To treat all Sikhs as brothers and service to the community and country as their first duty. (4) To abstain from liquor, intoxicants and tobacco. (5) To live by honest means and respect the wives of others. (6) To worship one God (Timeless Lord of all). (7) To have no faith in magic, charms and believe in community organisation. (8)To promote education, arts and to give ten percent from personal savings in charity. (9) To accept Guru Gobind Singh as father and Mata Sahib Kaur as mother, and all those who have received Guru's Amrit as brothers. (10) To practise the use of arms and ready to sacrifice all for the sake of the Guru Panth.

When the candidates agree to observe the above rules, the five selected Singhs (Panj Payaras), proceed to prepare the Amrit. Some sugar or puffed sugar is mixed in clean water in an iron bowl. The five Singhs sit around the iron bowl and each of them by turn holds the iron bowl within his left hand and stirs the water and sugar with a double-edged-dagger, breathing into the mixture the magic of Guru's word. First the senior brother recites the full text of the Japji Sahib; the second Singh sitting next to him takes the dagger and stirred the sugared mixture while reading the Japji Sahib of Guru Gobind. The third hands over the dagger to the fourth who stirs the mixture with it, and reads a chaupai from the evening prayer, in the end the fifth takes the dagger and recites Anand Sahib given in the evening prayer. When he has finished, the Amrit (nectar for baptism) is ready and the senior brother administers the Amrit to the candidates who have been standing and reading the Japji Sahib. Each recipient of Amrit is made to sit in Vir Asan (sitting with his left knee down and righrt knee up). The senior brother asks the candidates to say (Wahe Guru Ji Ka Khalsa Sri Wahe Guru Ji Ki Fatah) (The Khalsa- pure Sikh, is of God and to God is the victory). The process is repeated five times and the Amrit is sprinked on their face and eyes, and some of it given to the candidates to drink from the palm of their hands, exclaiming (Wahe Guru Ji Ka Khalsa Wahi Guru Ji Ki Fatah). After the Amrit has been given, the ceremony is concluded by all partaking of Karah Prasad (consecrated food), which is distributed in equal proportions to the entire congregation irrespective of caste or status.

Karah Parshad ceremony

From the time of Guru Nanak the practice of a common kitchen for the whole congregation has been the rule. Free food is given to every person who would come to eat in the Gurdwara. Karah Parshad is a specially prepared halwa. The person who prepares it is a Sikh and he should repeat Japji Sahib while preparing Karah Parshad. It is made from wheat flour (Suji), clarified butter and Sugar; all three in equal quantities in weight. To this is added pure water equal to the combined weight of all the three ingredients. First sugar is dissolved in water and placed on a fire to simmer, in an iron pan. When the syrup comes to a boiling point, then flour (Suji) is added to it and stirred so that no balls are formed. When the flour is thoroughly cooked, its colour is changed slightly brownish and smells like freshly cooked biscuits. At this stage the syrup is mixed into it and the Halwa or Karah Parshad is ready. Before the congregation disperses after the prayer ceremonies, the Karah Parshad is served in equal quantities to every one.

Arranged Marriage

In early times, the selection of the bride and the groom was mutual either from love or other considerations, and in majority of the cases love formed the dominant factor. In India marriages are arranged in the sense that a boy and a girl is introduced to each other by their families, but the boy and the girl has the final choice and not the head of the family. In villages it is still possible that their parents or their families choose the husband or wife. Sometimes the relations who can also give a binding promise of betrothal are: father, mother, grandfather and brother of the bride.

In every case it is made sure that the bride and groom are well suited to each other in terms of age, personality, education, economic status, respectable family background, good character and health, free from hereditary disease, and are both sound in body and mind.

When all these points have been investigated, an auspicious day is fixed for the engagement. After this girl's parents, relations and friends go to the boy's house at the fixed appointment to give Sagun (presents of clothes, jewellery, dry fruits, fresh fruits, sweets etc.) to the boy and his family. The girl's family members wish the groom good luck, happiness, and prosperity in married life, and also meaning that we will accept the boy as a member of our family. Accordingly the boy, his family, some relations and friends would also go to the bride's house for the ceremony. At present engagement usually happens within the month of the marriage, but it can happen earlier as well. This ceremony usually happens with sacred music and chanting of sacred verses from the Vedas or Guru Granth Sahib. It is believed in Hinduism and Sikhism that a house will only prosper if the women of the household are respected. Therefore the groom must pay his respects to the bride.

At the girl's house the boy's father request the girl's father, "Give your daughter to my son." The girl's father after consulting his family says: I give this girl, born in such and such family, daughter of such and such person and namely so and so to your son. My daughter has been given by us orally to your son and accepted by you. After the proposal has been accepted the father of the groom and other members of his family accept the girl with flowers and presents of clothes, jewellery, make-up things, sweets etc. The boy gives an engagement ring to the girl as a life long loyalty and commitment to each other. A large part of the fruits and sweets are distributed to girl's family friends and relations to announce that the marriage has been fixed.

By this ceremony the bridegroom and his family are tied down to the engagement and marriage on a pre-fixed date. When once the promise of engagement has passed the lips of the girl's parents, it can only be withdrawn for grave causes.

Marriage ceremonies

Maiyan

Seven or eight days before the date of the marriage, the bride and bridegroom are supposed to be confined to their houses. They cannot go out of their houses until the marriage day. This is called Maiyan or Sahe baithna. This is obviously a precaution against accidents, but it is also probably intended to avoid exposure to the sun and to enhance the beauty on the wedding day as far as possible. With this in view, both parties have to rub oil all over the body every morning, after which they are sponged with a mixture of flour and ghee called batna before taking their baths.

Ghorian

Ghorian literally means 'of the mare', that is songs sung by the sisters and relatives of the bridegroom, who riding a mare proceeds to the house of the bride for his wedding ceremony. Many times vulgar and nasty folk songs are sung on this occasion. Guru Ram Das wrote two hymns of four verses each in Rag Waddhans (GGS p.575) under this heading.

In the first hymn, he compares the human body to a mare.

Just as the mare is decorated with a fine harness and saddle, in the same way, the human body needs the harness of Divine Name so that it can travel safely in the difficult world. Mind can be controlled with the reigns of spiritual knowledge and the whip of love. God has arranged the marriage of the individual soul with the Supreme Soul. The procession consists of holy men and wise companions who will help the union of man with God.

In the second hymn (GGS. p. 576) The Guru elaborated the theme. The golden-bodied steed needs to be decorated with a golden harness studded with the gems of Holy Name. God blesses one with joy and bliss as he keeps Him sincerely in his heart. The Guru has controlled the elephant like mind with reigns and whip and as such the mind has become stable and imbued with God's presence. The bride is overflowing with love for her Lord and will find lasting happiness in his company. The body is a vehicle for union with the Supreme Being, but it is through the wisdom of the Guru that man will get in tune with the Infinite. Blessed is the human birth, which leads to this Divine consummation.

Milni

Milni (meeting) takes places when the wedding party reaches the bride's house for the marriage. The bridegroom's father and a few close relatives are introduced to the bride's father and her close relatives who give gifts to the father of the bridegroom and other close relatives in the shape of a present. At the same time the procession is served some refreshments.

Anand Karaj (Marriage)

A Sikh marriage is called an Anand Karaj. In the past a Sikh marriage was celebrated according to the ordinary Hindu rites, performed by Brahmans, with the only difference being that hymns of the fourth Guru (Ramdas) were sung simultaneously by the females during the ceremony in place of the Hindi songs. Later, a dual ceremony was adopted whereby the Hindu rites were performed first, and then the wedded couple circumambulated the Granth Sahib four times, while the Sikh priest reads lavan hymns. The Sikhs of modern times have, however, completely given up the Hindu ritual and content themselves with the circumambulation of the Granth Sahib, and the reading of hymns by the Sikh priest. The lavan, which are a counterpart of the four pheras (going round the sacrificial fire by the Hindus) but known to the Sikhs, as Parikramas constitute the binding part of the ceremony.

The marriage usually starts with singing of Asa Di Var (ballad of hope). It is a composition of Guru Nanak and Guru Angad in the Guru Granth Sahib. The theme of Asa Di Var is how to become spiritual person (devta). First musicians (Ragis) sing the following Shabad seeking grace of the Guru.

Kita lorhiye kam su hari pahi akhiye
Karju deye svahi, Satigur sachi akhiye
Santa sangi nidhan, amrita chkhiye,
Bhai bhanjan mirahavan, das ki chakhiye
Nanak Hari gun gaiye, alakh prabh lakhiye

It means: before undertaking anything seek the grace of god. By the grace of the Guru, success is obtained, who is in the company of the saints, and who expounds the truth. It is with the true Guru that we tasted ambrosia. O merciful god showers your grace on your servant. Nanak says that by praising God we understand the infinite.

The priest explains the concept of Sikh marriage and utters the following words of Guru Amar Das on page 788 of the Adi Granth.

The bride should know no other man except her own husband. One who is adorned with love of her husband shines. To be humble and true to his bidding is the only way to beloved's heart. They are not man and wife who have physical contact only. Only those are truly wedded who have one spirit in two bodies.

Guru Arjan Dev also tells the bride how to win the heart of her husband—by sweetness of speech and beauty of contentment. A loaf of dry bread and bed of bare earth is full of happiness in the company of beloved. Let humility be the word, contentment the offering, the tongue be the mint of sweetness. If you adopt these, then you will have him in your power. Then the couple bow towards the Guru Granth Sahib.

The Sikh wedding ceremony takes place in the presence of the Sikh holy book, the Guru Granth Sahib. The Sikh marriage ceremony initiated by Guru Amardas (third Guru) for the Sikh community consists of the recitation of Anand Sahib (therefore called Anand Karaj). Later on, Guru Ramdas added the lavan (wedding song) for recitation and singing. The Sikh marriage ceremony was given statutory recognition by the Anand Marriage Act of 1909 of the Indian government. The details of the marriage ceremony will be found in the Rahat-Maryada booklet published by the SGPC, Amritsar. However a summary of the ceremony is given below. The Anand ceremony is a sacrament, but the marriage may be dissolved under the divorce law of the state. Widows and widowers can also be married through this ceremony. Monogamy is practised by the Sikhs. Caste distinctions and giving of dowry are discouraged.

Granth Sahib, is placed on an altar under a canopy. All guests take their shoes off and cover their heads before entering the hall where the ceremony is going to take place. Everyone proceeds towards the altar, places a monetary offering as token of respect and bows to the scripture. (Guests of other faiths who choose not to proceed towards the altar may remain seated after entering the hall). Everyone sits cross-legged on the floor.

After the hymns are sung, the groom comes forward and takes his place facing the front of the altar. The bride then joins the congregation and sits on the left side of the groom. Whoever is conducting the marriage asks the couple and their parents to stand whilst he or she prays to God to bless the marriage. A short hymn is then sung which contains the general advice: "Before undertaking anything seek the Grace of GodÖ" (GGS, p. 91). The priest or an official explains the meaning of the Sikh marriage: marriage is not a social contract but aims at the fusion of two souls into one. It is analogous to the union of God and man, which is the goal of Sikh piety. Various hymns give advice on marriage which imply:

The bride should know no other man except her husband, so the Guru ordains. She alone is of a good family; she alone shines with light that is adorned with the love of her husband. Only they are truly wedded who have one spirit in two bodies. . . . (GGS, p. 788).

The bride and the groom publicly assent to the marriage by bowing towards the Guru Granth Sahib. When they have sat down, the bride's father comes forward and places one end of the scarf that hangs from the groom's shoulder in the hand of his daughter. After a short hymn is sung, the officiate opens the Sikh scripture on page 773 of the GGS and begins to read the lavan of Guru Ramdas. The first verse is read and then sung as the couple walk slowly round the Guru Granth Sahib in a clockwise direction, the groom leading. They return to their places and sit down. Three more verses are read and the circling is repeated in the same fashion. The last is often a signal for the throwing of flower-petals at the couple. The service concludes with the singing of the first five and last verses of the Anand Sahib followed by the prayer (ardas). The Guru's Hukam (vak) is taken by opening the scripture at random and the congregation is served with Karah Prasaad (sacrament). A meal usually follows the ceremony before the bride and groom leave to begin their new life.

Anand Sahib—recited at the end of every Sikh wedding

Anand Sahib is a poetical composition of Guru Amardas included in the Guru Granth Sahib. It consists of 40 stanzas. The work "Anand" means permanent joy and bliss. Worldly power, wealth and position do not give joy or happiness; on the contrary, they produce fear, tension, pride and loss of peace of mind. The ideal goal of man is spiritual fulfilment or being in tune with the Infinite.

The hurdles in the spiritual path are egoism, family attachments, chain of desire, hypocrisy and social compulsions, and they can be controlled by following the instructions of the Guru. Bliss is attained through self-discipline and the development of one's own personality through contentment, compassion, morality and social service.

The Anand assures everyone that he can experience tranquillity and peace of mind without sacrificing the normal comforts and pleasures of life. Bliss is the ultimate destiny of man. Pain and suffering, though unavoidable, do not disturb the inner peace of that person who leads a pious life according to the Guru's instructions contained in the sacred hymns. Anand Sahib is composed in Ramkali Raga, which leaves a powerful impression on the mind. The diction is felicitous, its "winged" words and "pregnant" phrases clearly explain difficult concepts like Shaj, Hukum, Amrit, Nirmal, Sansa, Punn, Maya, etc.

The Anand Sahib is recited at the end of every Sikh wedding service in its abbreviated form (first five and last stanzas). It is also recited or sung at the end of every religious service before ardas (prayer) and thereafter Hukam is taken and Karah Parsaad (consecrated pudding) is distributed among the congregation.

Lavan

Lavan is the name of a composition of four verses by Guru Ramdas in Rag Suhi on page 773 (GGS), and it was composed as a wedding song for the Sikhs. These verses are recited twice; first by the Granthi, and sung when the couple go round the Holy Granth. The purpose of repetition is to stress upon the couple to relate their married life to the spiritual goal of the life mentioned in the Lavan.

The first verse of the lavan, mentions the performance of duties in married life. Household life is a training school where we learn to overcome selfishness and begin to love and serve others. The couple is enjoined to maintain the household and family life and discharge its duties and obligations. They must give up sin, which includes greed and adultery and also practice righteousness and contentment. Marriage is not a commercial transaction or contract and as such, dowry is discouraged.

The second verse emphasises the need of following the Sikh way of life—Rahatmaryada—and the Guru's teaching. The husband and the wife can derive from Gurbani the moral strength to avoid sin and to feel the presence of God in his manifold creation.

The third verse emphasises non-attachment and consequent joy in the midst of worldly temptations. Both must cultivate the virtue of detachment and egolessness. This will lead the couple to the ultimate enlightenment.

The fourth verse describes the stage of peace and bliss. One will then cease to be disturbed by joy or sorrow, and feel the presence of God both in and around oneself. Such a person will have no fear and no worry, for his mind is stable and contented. This promotes the spirit of resignation to the Will of God and builds up one's patience. These verses thus sum up the values and virtues of the ideal married life, as a journey towards perfection and salvation.

The literal translation of Lavan (wedding song) is as follows:

First round. In the first round, the Lord ordains for you a secular life.

The scriptures are the word of the Lord, learn righteousness through them, and the Lord will free you from sin.

Let your law of life be to meditate on the Name of God, which is the theme of all scriptures.

Contemplate the true and perfect Guru, and all your sins shall depart.

Fortunate are those who hold God in their hearts; they are ever serene and happy.

The slave Nanak declares that in the first round the marriage ceremony has begun.

Second round. In the second round, the Lord has caused you to meet the True Guru.

The fear in your hearts has departed, and the filth of egoism has been washed away.

By having the fear of God and singing his praises, you behold His very presence.

The God is the soul of the universe, and His presence pervades everywhere.

Know then that there is one God, within us and without, and in the company of the saints; the songs of joy are sung. The servant Nanak proclaims, that in the second round, divine music is heard.

Third round. In the third round there is longing for the Lord and detachment from the world.

In the company of the saints and by great good fortune you have come to meet the Lord.

Singing his praises and speaking the Divine word God can be found..

By great good fortune, we have taken the company of the saints, and told the story of the ineffable Lord.

The holy name echoes in the heart and absorbs us.

We repeat the name of the Lord, being blessed by a fortunate destiny, the slave Nanak declares that in the third round, Divine love is born in the heart.

Fourth round. In the fourth round the mind grasps the knowledge of the Divine, and union with God is complete.

Through the grace of the union is made easy.

The sweetness of the Beloved, pervades us body and soul.

Dear and pleasing is the Lord to us, and we remain ever absorbed in Him.

By singing the Lord's praises I have attained, the object of my heart's desire – my Lord.

God has completed this marriage, and the bride rejoices in His name.

The humble Nanak proclaims that in the fourth round, you have obtained God, as the everlasting Bridegroom.

Some of the miscellaneous ceremonies connected with Anand marriage are as follows:

Jai Mala

It is the ceremony in which the bride and groom exchange garlands, thus signifying their bond together.

Vari and Khat

Vari is the name given to the ornaments and clothes made by the parents of the boy for the bride. Khat is the ceremony in which the parents of the girl give cash, ornaments, utensils, and clothes to the parents of the boy. This ceremony is performed during the day of the actual marriage itself while the wedding party is still in the house of the bride before starting back.

Chadar ceremony

This is a ceremony among the Sikhs, of marrying a widow to a brother or other near relative of the deceased husband, which consists in having a single sheet spread over the contracting parties by the officiating Granthi (priest). The priest says some hymns and pronounce them husband and wife.

Dastar-Bandi/Turban ceremony

This is the ceremony of tying the turban. Generally when an elderly male person who is the head of the family dies, the community or neighbours formally tie a turban to the eldest son in the family in token of his having taken over the new responsibility of the family of the dead person. Also the ceremony is held for a Sikh boy in his teens, with his wearing of the turban for the first time to indicate his commitment to the Sikh faith.

In medieval times both the Hindus and Sikhs generally used turbans. The Sikhs wear their turbans because they maintain unshorn hair. The turban keeps their hair free of dust and dirt and keeps it out of the way so that they can do their daily work comfortably. The last Guru Gobind Singh forbids them to cut their hair. All the things, which are bad for the health of the body, including drinking and smoking, are banned. In the Rahatnama of Guru Gobind Singh it is mentioned that a Sikh should not wear cap/hat/topi, and it is forbidden to take off the turbans while eating. The turban has become an identification mark for the Sikhs. The Sikhs can wear turbans of any colour, but the Akalis wear blue turbans, the Nihangs wear yellow and Kukas/ Namdhari wear white. Many Sikh children cover their topknot with a handkerchief till they are able to tie their own turbans. Some Sikhs also wear an under-turban to prevent their outer turban soiling with hair oil. The Sikh women do not generally wear turbans, and cover their head with a scarf or dupatta. Some American Sikh females and Akhand-Kirtani Jatha women do wear turbans.

Birth customs and ceremonies

During pregnancy no rites are observed amongst Sikh women except that great precautions are taken during the Solar and Lunar eclipses. Usually elderly women believe that a pregnant woman is not supposed to work during an eclipse and is often not allowed even to move, as it is believed that any movement of the mother is likely to affect the appearance of the child. Before childbirth, purgatives and laxative food are avoided, especially in the advanced stages. In villages, and wherever possible, in the first few days after delivery the parents of the girl send some punjiri for their girl, and ornaments and clothes for the child. Punjiri is a confection of ghi, sugar, almonds, flour, raisins, dates, coconut, etc. fried in a pan, is a very favourite dish after childbirth Amongst the Sikh, the mother in villages, is confined to a room for a period of thirteen days, after which there is no restriction to leaving the house. For the first five days strict seclusion is observed. All these precautions are taken to prevent the evil influence of malevolent spirits, although they may have been originally on hygienic principles. A lamp is kept burning throughout the night, and a little fire is kept smouldering in the room to drive off evil spirits, really serves to disinfect the air.

The birth of a son is the occasion of great rejoicing, but in some families the birth of a daughter is not an occasion of rejoicing. On the eve of the 13th day the families of the family clean the whole of the house, clothes are washed, all the utensils in the house are cleaned. On the 13th, or any odd day after birth, a name is given to the child.

Naming ceremony

Some families distribute sweets on the birth of a child (male/female), and it is believed that men and women are equal in the eyes of God. Usually in villages the birth of a son is the occasion of great rejoicing in contradistinction to that of a daughter. On the birth of a child some elder member of the family pour some water into a bowl, an iron or silver bowl if possible, and add some honey into it. The mixture will be stirred with a Khanda or a spoon while reciting some verses from Guru Nanak's Japji. A few drops of this mixture are poured into the baby's mouth. The same ceremony may be repeated in their local Gurdwara before the Holy Granth.

On the 13th, or any odd day after birth, a name is given to the child. The Granthi or any elder member of the family opens the Guru Granth Sahib at random. The first letter of the first line on the left hand page, at which the book opens, must be the initial letter of the name bestowed on the infant. Thus if "I" is the first letter above described, any of the names Indra, Indrajit may be given. The suffix Singh is usually added at the baptism (Pahul) ceremony. After the Amrit (holy water) has been given, the ceremony is concluded by all partaking of Karah Parshad (consecrated food), which is distributed in equal proportions to the entire congregation.

Wedding anniversaries

Most couples like to celebrate wedding anniversaries with presents and a good meal in a restaurant etc. Traditionally certain materials are associated with individual years in the course of a marriage, the idea being that anniversary presents in those years should be made out of those particular materials.

The list below gives the materials generally associated with each year.

Anniversary	Wedding
First	Cotton or paper
Second	Paper
Third	Leather
Fourth	Silk or flowers
Fifth	Wood
Sixth	Sugar
Seventh	Wool or copper
Eighth	Bronze
Ninth	Pottery
Tenth	Tin
Eleventh	Steel
Twelfth	Silk and fine linen or leather
Thirteenth	Lace
Fourteenth	Ivory
Fifteenth	Crystal
Twentieth	Chine
Twenty-fifth	Silver
Thirtieth	Pearl
Thirty-fifth	Coral
Fortieth	Ruby
Forty-fifth	Sapphire
Fiftieth	Gold
Fifty-fifth	Emerald
Sixtieth	Diamond
Seventieth	Platinum
Seventy-fifth	Diamond

Changing your surname

A professional woman does not have to change her surname when she gets married, although it is generally expected and usually makes life a little easier when making joint social, legal or financial arrangements. If you do decide to change your name the following authorities should be the first one to be notified:

> Employer, bank, building society, saving accounts, insurance companies, credit card companies, passport office (it is convenient if you change name on your passport), Inland Revenue, Department of Health and Social Security, DVLC (Driver's Licence and Vehicle Registration Document), Doctor and Dentist.

Divorce

Marriage among Sikhs is a sacrament and as such there can be no divorce from the religious point of view. However, divorce is possible under the law, since Sikhs are classified as Hindus under the Indian law, divorce is permissible under the Hindu marriage Act of 1955. Sikhs can get divorce in India on certain grounds like change of religion, cruelty, insanity, venereal disease, leprosy, adultery, impotence and desertion. The courts have the right to decide on the question of maintenance and the custody of children. After divorce either of the couple can contract a marriage.

Funeral ceremony

When a person is about to die his or her attention is drawn towards God and no sorrow should be allowed to intrude upon a peaceful death. As soon a person has died the body should be bathed and clothed in clean clothes and removed to a place for cremation. The practice of weeping, crying and showing grief are strictly forbidden. As the funeral procession moves the hymns from Sohi of Ravidas may be recited, which means that all human beings are guests on this earth, and everyone born has died, and you must go as well, and so on.

At the cremation ground the body is placed on top of a platform of firewood and general prayer is recited, and blessings of God and the Guru are invoked for the peace and happiness of the departed soul. After cremation the party of mourners return to the deceased house and wash their hands and faces or take a complete bath and wear new clothes, and after that Karah Parshad is distributed. The idea is that there should be no grief shown at the passing away of the soul from the earth, as it is a natural process just like birth. As soon as it is convenient, the reading of the Holy Granth Sahib takes place in the house of the deceased and the reading is completed on the tenth day, when with final prayers for the departed soul takes place, and the funeral ceremony closes.

Sikh – geographical limits of occupation or influence

During the sixteenth and seventeenth centuries Guru Nanak and other Gurus, of the Kshatriya race, obtained many converts to their doctrines of religious reforms in Hinduism and social emancipation among the Jat peasants of Lahore and the southern banks of the Sutlej River. This reform movement in Hinduism became very popular. The Sikhs (learners or disciples) of the Gurus occupied or extended their influence from Delhi to Peshawar, and the plains of Sind to the Karakoram mountains. The dominions acquired by the Sikhs are thus included between the 28th and 36th parallels of north latitude, and between the 71st and 77th meridians of east longitude; and if a base of four hundred and fifty miles be drawn from Panipat to the Khaibar Pass, two triangles, almost equivalent, may be described upon it, which shall include the conquests of Ranjit Singh and the fixed colonies of the Sikh people.

Banda Bahadur or Banda Bairagi (Saint) (1670-1716) was born in a Rajput family in Poonch (Kashmir) on 27 October 1670. He became a follower of Guru Gobind Singh. He enlisted a number of soldiers and attacked Panjab and became the ruler of some parts of Panjab and established his capital at Lohgarh near Sandhura and became a very popular ruler. He brought the country between Lahore and Jammu under Sikh control.

Reform movements in Hinduism started with Jainism and Buddhism. Ramanuja in 12th century became a very popular reformer. His disciple Ramananda became very popular in

13th and 14th centuries. Kabir, Raidas, Sena, Pipa, Mira Bai and Guru Nanak followed the reform tradition and helped Ramananda in his mission. Guru Nanak became very successful in Northern India. Nanak thus a name of usual occurrence, both among Hindus and Muhammadans. In olden days it was common in many parts of. India that women used to choose their own parents home as the place of their confinement, especially of their first child, and the children thus born are frequently called Nanak or Nanake (in the feminine), from the word Nanke (one's mother's parents).

The strength of the Sikhs is estimated by the unity and energy of the religious fervour and warlike temperament. They are very hardy and have always looked forward to their success against Muslims, Afghans and Arabs. The declension of the Sikh Kashatriyas from soldiers and sovereigns into traders and shopkeepers has a parallel in the history of the Jews.

Index